MARIANNE MOORE

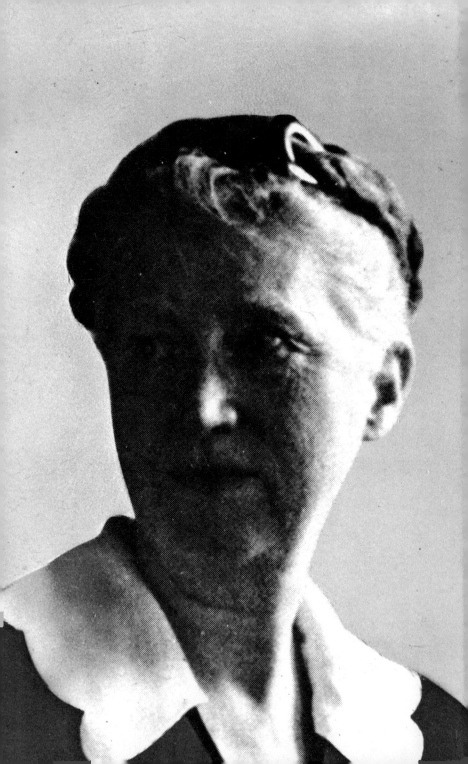

MARIANNE MOORE

❧ ❧

THE CAGE AND THE ANIMAL

❧ ❧

DONALD HALL

PEGASUS   NEW YORK

Marianne Moore is part of a series, Pegasus American
Authors, prepared under the General Editorship of
Richard M. Ludwig, Princeton University.

To Zoe and Joe Pearson

✌ CONTENTS

❧ ACKNOWLEDGMENTS

I am most grateful to Norman Holmes Pearson, who read this book in manuscript and made many helpful suggestions and corrections. Judith Johnson was invaluable to me, in her checking and other editorial assistance. Elizabeth Cooper contributed to the writing of this book more than I am able to acknowledge. The errors are my own. Of course I am highly indebted to Miss Moore's own statements, in my earlier interviews with her.

CHAPTER I ❧ INTRODUCTION

❧ *IN THE SPRING* of 1969, Marianne Moore received an honorary degree from Harvard. A year earlier she had opened the baseball season at Yankee Stadium, tossing out the first ball at the invitation of the owners. In neither case was it necessary to introduce Miss Moore to her audience, for long before she reached the age of eighty she had become a legend. People who have never read a poem recognize Miss Moore on the street in her wide black cape and black tricorn hat. Her comments provide copy for journalists, more for their manner than for their matter. She is a licensed eccentric whose affection for the vanished Brooklyn Dodgers is renowned.

Equally, Miss Moore has become a legend to those people who *do* read poetry. This is too bad. To be legendary is often to be dismissed. Enduring fame can be a kind of pigeonhole. Marianne Moore's is a pleasant pigeonhole: among critics she is almost universally admired. The unanimity of affectionate respect is, in fact, remarkable; no one whose poetry is being read with close attention could be held in such unvarying esteem. One suspects that, in a curious way, Miss Moore has, indeed, been dismissed. Long since, she has been read, "understood," and accorded a permanent pedestal.

She deserves better treatment. Being understood is a condition fatal to further understanding. When Marianne Moore is unanimously acclaimed a technical virtuoso, everything important is left unsaid. She is recognized as a master of surface perfections whose poems are difficult, intelligent, scrupulously accurate and charmingly whimsical. There is at the same time general agreement that they are unemotional. As early as 1935, T. S. Eliot was defending Marianne Moore's work against charges of frigidity. That emotion was not immediately apparent did not mean that it was absent, he claimed.[1] Yet the idea that the poetry lacks feeling persists. Miss Moore's reputation rests on brilliant surfaces and on charming eccentricities.

The basis for this reputation is understandable. The surface of the poems *is* brilliant. Miss Moore's poetic technique has reached its own potential. One may read such a poem as "The Jerboa" and be convinced that if surface is all, it is enough. But in limiting one's understanding of Miss Moore's poetry to an appreciation of polished surfaces, too much is ignored. How does one explain a poem like "A Grave" by applying to surfaces? One would have to ignore the dark music of feeling that informs that poem; the sacrifice would be too great.

Critics insist on the brilliance of Miss Moore's surfaces and, after all, the surfaces are there. It is Miss Moore who has created them, so part of the insistence, then, must be her own. A polished surface can serve as a concealment. Reflecting light, it can deflect attention from what it conceals. In numbers of Miss Moore's early poems, I think her concentration upon technique, wit, and intellectual hair-splitting serves such a purpose. A young woman's vulnerable feelings hide behind the cleverness. In the poems of her middle years, Miss Moore is less concerned with high polish (although the decreased concern is only relative) but often the content of the poetry is more conventional. In such a poem as "What Are Years?" the feelings expressed, although strongly stated, are those not-very-private ones that any thoughtful person might have in considering human life. The surface may be penetrable because the feelings are acceptably conventional. In the first sort of poem, feeling is controlled by a manipulation of surface fireworks. In the second kind, the feeling itself is a surface. It is ordinary emotion, rationally expressed.

Throughout the poetry, from early to late, there is a third kind of poem that interests me most. It not only deals with the content lurking deep under the surfaces but is expressed in images that come from these depths. Such a poem is "A Grave." There are others like "The Plumet Basilisk," "The Fish," "Marriage," and "Sun." These are poems in which the ostensible subject—the surface object—simply will not support the weight of implied concern. Something else, something quite different from the stated subject, is in control of the poem.

In one of Miss Moore's early poems, "Novices," she speaks of "sea-serpented regions / 'unlit by the half-lights of more conscious art.'" It is from this dark place that poetry derives. Early in her career, then, Miss Moore was aware of the "sea-serpented" place and its importance to poetry. A great deal of her subsequent work can be seen as an effort to reach and survive contact with this perilous region. She recognized its treasures but she knew, too, the emotional dangers inherent in its darknesses.

Miss Moore's surfaces, then, are not perfected simply for their own sake. It is almost axiomatic that in Marianne Moore's poetry the more glittering the surface, the greater the underlying emotion. The stronger and more frightening the feeling, the more necessary the protection that complexity of surface can provide. In the third category of poem I mention, the surface dazzles. The poems are rooms of mirrors, faceted with imagery that blinds in its brilliance. They have an Arabian Nights opulence held tightly in a frame of technical control.

Something peculiar happens intermittently in these poems. In the midst of comprehensibility, rational content suddenly disappears. All at once there is no paraphrasable meaning. Nothing makes sense. One realizes slowly that something else has taken over the poem. The images are no longer images of any *thing* but are, rather, images of feeling. They are molten, coming like lava from the dark place of serpents and gold. The surface has broken and the crazy language of the unconscious mind pours in. Here is a passage from "Sun":

O Sun, you shall stay
  with us; holiday,
    consuming wrath, be wound in a device
of Moorish gorgeousness, round glasses spun
  to flame as hemispheres of one
great hour-glass dwindling to a stem.

It would be impossible to give a rational paraphrase of these
lines. Their meaning is not available to the rational mind,
nor were the words derived from reason.

It is these moments when control is lost, these eruptions
of feeling, that are for me the greatest pleasure in Marianne
Moore's poetry. The surface of the poetry is undeniably
brilliant, but it is perhaps the power of underlying emotion
that is responsible for its highly-worked perfection. Throughout much of Miss Moore's work we feel the struggle of feeling to be born. Feeling is both resisted and desired in a ten-
sion of yielding and control. When Miss Moore writes, "Nor
was he insincere in saying, 'Make my house your inn.' / Inns
are not residences" it is with superb control. When she writes,
"Below the incandescent stars / below the incandescent fruit, /
the strange experience of beauty; / its existence is too much; /
it tears one to pieces / and each fresh wave of consciousness /
is poison" she is floating on feeling. I would not choose to
sacrifice one thing and keep the other. It would, in fact, be
impossible to *have* the one without the other. But it seems
reasonable to me, when encountering such a display of precision
and control, to wonder what needs controlling and to search
in the poems for a strength of emotion equal to the effort
made to restrain it.

People who have chosen to see only the surfaces of Marianne Moore's poetry have missed at least half of what is
there. In calling attention to technical detail so determinedly
they have fallen into the trap the poet, herself, has provided;
they have taken her insistence upon emotional restraint as
evidence of no emotion. There is enormous restraint, of course,
but one should not be misled by it. Only the wildest animals
need cages so carefully made.

CHAPTER II ❧ CHILDHOOD

❧ *MARIANNE MOORE* was born on November 15, 1887, in Kirkwood, Missouri, a suburb of St. Louis. She was the second child of Mary and John Milton Moore. Her brother John had been born seventeen months earlier. Miss Moore can scarcely remember her father, who was an engineer. Together with his brother, he had designed and planned to manufacture a smokeless furnace. When the plans failed he suffered a nervous breakdown and returned to his parents' home in Portsmouth, Ohio, leaving his family in Kirkwood. They never saw him again.

Mrs. Moore, with her two children, moved into the house of her father, the Reverend John Riddle Warner, a Presbyterian minister in Kirkwood. They were a close and affectionate family. Invariably, Miss Moore has spoken with respect and love of her mother and her brother. They seem to have been essential supports in her life.

Mrs. Moore, one gathers, was a person somewhat like her daughter. Miss Moore thinks that she was a literary person without really being conscious of it. She had a respect for the precisions of language similar to her daughter's and was impatient with sloppy expression. She served as a critic of her daughter's poetry until her death in 1947, and Miss Moore invariably took her opinions about a poem to heart. Miss Moore confesses to having reached college so accustomed to sharing thoughts with her mother that she felt uncomfortable, almost incapable of undertaking work independently. She liked to discuss everything, to have her ideas corrected phrase by phrase. She thinks that she was brought up with almost too much attention, was "hand-reared." [1]

The Reverend Warner was pastor of the First Presbyterian Church in Kirkwood. The pastor of the Unitarian Church in the same small town was Dr. William Eliot, grandfather of T. S. Eliot. The two preachers met occasionally at ministerial gatherings but the families did not know each other. It seems uncanny that two of the best American poets of this century should have been born and lived within a few miles of one another. Later, they became important to each other. Eliot admired Miss Moore's poetry and wrote the Introduction to the English volume of her *Selected Poems* in 1935. But during childhood in St. Louis they were unaware of each other's existence.

Religion was, of necessity, important in the childhood of Marianne and of John Moore. John Moore went on to become a Presbyterian minister. Miss Moore has attended church regularly every Sunday of her life and has taken an interested and active part in church activities. A Christian upbringing can produce a sensitivity to mystery, to things of the spirit. To be attuned to mystery is to sense its presence in any of its guises; it is this sensitivity that informs Miss Moore's poetry.

Miss Moore's early years in Kirkwood were happy ones. She remembers her grandfather as an affectionate man; probably, he took the place of the missing father to a large extent. She had pets, kittens and puppies and an alligator, Tibby, whom she says she tended "as if he were a little deity." This was the first of Miss Moore's pet alligators. She had another one in the 1960s which she kept in her Brooklyn apartment.

She remembers parties in Kirkwood given by Mrs. E. P. Howard, a friend of her mother's who had been Mrs. Moore's classmate at St. Louis' Mary Institute. They were "scintillating" affairs to this little red-haired girl, complete with "spun-sugar candy and favors." The same friend took the children for rides in a brougham pulled by two horses with cropped tails to see swan boats on the lake, "like the ones there are in Boston." Later, after the Moores had moved from Kirkwood, the same friend sent Christmas boxes for each of them. Miss Moore remembers them as a mélange of festive and imaginative presents.

In 1894 the Reverend Warner died. Mrs. Moore took her two children and moved to Carlisle, Pennsylvania, where she had family. To the young Marianne Moore, she has later said, journeys always meant funerals. As the family was setting out for Pennsylvania, she asked her mother, "Is this a funeral?" She was too young to be much upset by the move, she thinks, but one wonders how it must have been to have lost two fathers by the age of seven.

In Carlisle, Mrs. Moore supported her children on a small inheritance and by teaching English for a time at the Metzger Institute, a girls' school that has since become incorporated into Dickinson College. The family lived at 343 North Hanover Street and Miss Moore remembers, or, perhaps more accurately, is willing to talk about, only a few external details of the time and place. There were Mennonites nearby, a Hessian guardhouse and a mermaid weathervane. There was a brick in the garden walk imprinted with a cat's paw. The garden was full of yellow flowers. Miss Moore still keeps the brick in her apartment and she has kept the flowers, too, less literally, in her poem, "Injudicious Gardening."

There were wonderful Thanksgiving dinners in Carlisle. Christmas, too, is a happy memory. The house was decorated with holly and ground pine and Mrs. Moore always bought a little hemlock tree covered with tiny cones until one year John, aged nine or ten, objected that the little tree could then not grow any more. After that there was holly and pine, but Mrs. Moore could not bring herself to have another tree.

Marianne Moore went to high school in Carlisle. She remembers particularly art courses that she liked, classes in drawing—milkweed pods and the Discobolus from a plaster cast. Painting has been an enduring interest. Miss Moore wanted to be a painter when she graduated from college. She continues to draw and paint from time to time for her own amusement or to illustrate something for herself that she wants to remember. In Carlisle she entered her paintings at the county fair and won prizes. She remembers calling for her prize money at the courthouse; one dollar or, perhaps, two.

She took Latin in a Latin class of two and found it difficult. She took German and apparently found that difficult as well. It seems curious that a person so gifted with language should have found courses in languages hardest throughout her school years. Drawing and painting were easier. Later biology was easier. All the raw material of her poetic imagery preceded her attempts to write, but when she began to write it was with the eye of a painter and the dissecting interest of a biologist.

Miss Moore entered Bryn Mawr in 1905. She had no literary plans, failed German immediately, then Italian twice. Eventually she passed them both, but says that she was at sea for two years. She was terribly homesick at first and in terror of some of her less sympathetic instructors. "I seemed to need very humane handling," she has said, "mothering by everyone—the case all my life, I think." Miss Moore's poetry reflects her timidity at the same time that it exhibits her considerable strength. Her need for mothering appears in the countless poems where protection is the subject and the amorphous inner and outer dangers of being alive are the threat. As in the poems, protection finally becomes a steeling of oneself, so at Bryn Mawr inner strength was what Miss Moore used finally to cope with her confusion.

She elected courses in biology because her grade standing in English was not high enough to entitle her to choose electives in that subject until her junior or senior year. She spent hours in the biology laboratory. She found the courses exhilarating and, in fact, briefly considered studying medicine. The precision, the drawing and identifying, the economy of statement and logic used for disinterested ends appealed to her. She thinks now that these methods of scientific study had a bearing on liberating her imagination. Certainly one can see evidence of this approach in her poetic style. Perhaps there really is, in applying the methods of scientific research to poetic construction, a liberating of the inner world of the imagination. Perhaps in keeping one's eye on technical detail one permits deeper content to slip in unguarded.

Even with biology Miss Moore had some trouble at first. The head of the department warned her that she must stop cutting classes, something she had never done. She told him that she would never think of cutting a class, was in deadly fear of missing something, that she was "just not grown up enough for these assignments; everyone is ahead of me. I seem a kind of juvenile." She took a class in torts because the professor of law from Columbia who taught the course seemed humane. He was a relief, she felt, from some of her more frightening instructors.

Finally, Miss Moore earned a grade average that entitled her to choose French and English electives. By then the only course available was seventeenth-century imitative writing— Francis Bacon, Jeremy Taylor, Launcelot Andrewes, Richard Hooker, and others. She enjoyed the course and found the antique sentence structure of the sermons appealing.

At the same time that she was having trouble academically, Miss Moore was beginning to write poems. She had poems printed in both the Bryn Mawr literary magazine, *Tipyn O'Bob,* and in the alumnae magazine, the *Lantern.* Of these poems, few have appeared in her mature collections. They are mostly exercises, academic imitations of various post-Victorian poets, prettified and romantic, and seem juvenile compared to even her earliest professional publications. Some of Miss Moore's later stylistic characteristics are evident in such poems as "Progress" and "Ennui," where the style is terse, almost abrupt.

The opening lines of "Ennui" are found nearly intact in a passage of "The Plumet Basilisk"; another poem, "To a Screen Maker," appears in her first book, *Poems,* as "He Made This Screen," but it is doubtful it would have appeared had Miss Moore been responsible for the selection of poems in that book. Only one poem from those early years at Bryn Mawr was published in a later volume. It is "Progress," which

appeared in 1959 in the collection, *O To Be A Dragon,* called
there, "I May, I Might, I Must." This poem, with its theme
of willed endurance, is particularly moving, I think, when one
knows that it was written during those confused and homesick years. Miss Moore printed thirteen poems in all in the
Bryn Mawr publications between 1907 and 1909. She was
elected to the board of *Tipyn O'Bob* in her sophomore year
and continued to serve during the rest of her stay at Bryn
Mawr.

There was another poet at Bryn Mawr during Miss Moore's
time there. She was Hilda Doolittle, who published her poems
later as H.D. She lived near the school, was a day student
and Miss Moore remembers her as having "wonderful grasshopper eyes."[2] H.D. was a friend of two other Philadelphians,
Ezra Pound and William Carlos Williams. Williams remembers that both he and Pound were half in love with H.D. at
that time and would take a trolley from Philadelphia to Bryn
Mawr to see her. He may, he thinks, have brushed by Marianne
Moore on one of those visits, but neither man really met her
until years later.

Miss Moore graduated with a Bachelor of Arts degree in
1909 and returned to Carlisle where she took a secretarial
course at Carlisle Commercial College. Then for three and a
half years, between 1911 and 1915, she taught typing, book-
keeping, stenography, commercial law, and commercial English at the United States Industrial Indian School in Carlisle.
She found the subjects uninspiring and does not think she
was a good teacher. She would much have preferred to stay
home reading.

One of Miss Moore's pupils at the Indian School was Jim
Thorpe, the famous Indian athlete. She remembers him as
gentle and chivalrous and calls him *James*—"He was always
James to me, nothing else." He was a slow student but he had
an astonishing decorum and wrote a fine Spencerian hand.
He was shy and polite. "Once," Miss Moore remembers, "we
were walking along railroad tracks in the heat. I had a gloria
man's umbrella. 'Could I carry your parasol for you?' he
said, 'Thank you, James,' I said, 'by all means.'"[3]

In the summer of 1911, July and August Miss Moore thinks, she and her mother made a trip abroad. They travelled mainly in England and visited Paris briefly, where they stayed on the Left Bank in a pension on the rue Valette. It was the place, Miss Moore remembers, where Calvin wrote his *Institutes* and was not far from the Luxembourg Gardens and the Pantheon. The two women went to every museum in Paris, Miss Moore recalls, "except two."

During these years Miss Moore continued writing poetry and began submitting her work to various magazines. In 1915, her first poem was published. The *Egoist*, a London journal edited by Richard Aldington and specializing in the then new Imagist verse, printed her "To the Soul of Progress," later called "To Military Progress." Aldington had married Miss Moore's classmate, H.D., and perhaps this accounts for the poem's finding its way to the English journal. Aldington always claimed later to have been Miss Moore's discoverer, a title contested by Alfred Kreymborg who, a year later, began publishing her poetry in his new journal, *Others*.

A month after the *Egoist* printed "To the Soul of Progress," *Poetry*, an American literary journal published in Chicago, printed five more poems by Marianne Moore. Harriet Monroe, *Poetry's* editor, had made her magazine the foremost journal for the young generation of American poets and Miss Moore's publication in *Poetry* amounted to considerable recognition of her talents. It established her as one of the new generation of innovators and brought her poetry to the attention of other poets working in new areas.

One poet who early recognized and praised the quality of Miss Moore's poetry was Ezra Pound. Although he, too, may have "brushed by" her at Bryn Mawr on a visit to H.D., it was not until her publications in the *Egoist* and *Poetry* that she came to his attention. In 1915, he wrote to Harriet Monroe praising the titles of Miss Moore's poems. By 1918, he was saying that Marianne Moore, together with Williams and some others, was a central figure in the new poetry. "Your stuff holds my eye," he wrote her. "O what about your age; how much more youngness is there to go into the work, and how much closening can be expected?" [4] He invited her to submit work for book publication and offered to help in arranging its contents.

Pound was one of many people who through the years that followed offered help and urged Miss Moore to publish her work. Although she claims to have been tenacious about submitting poems, her natural reticence must have tempered her tenacity enough to concern her admirers. Pound and Williams in particular pressed suggestions upon her. Eliot offered help. Miss Moore's first book was arranged and published by friends without her knowledge. In those early years she was a poet's poet, admired mainly by a very small group who could appreciate the newness of her work and who were willing to undertake the job of championing it.

Miss Moore does not say how it felt to be quite suddenly acclaimed by an important, if small, audience. She had read Pound's *The Spirit of Romance* and had admired it. She liked what she had read of Pound's poetry, though with reservations. It must have been enormously encouraging to have Pound's praise and to have the limited fame that followed the 1915 publications.

John Moore had graduated from Yale during this time and had been ordained, like his grandfather, a Presbyterian minister. In 1916, he was appointed pastor of the Ogden Memorial Church in Chatham, New Jersey. Miss Moore and her mother moved to Chatham that year to keep house for him. It was during this interlude in Chatham, between 1916 and 1918, that Marianne Moore began to print her poetry regularly in a variety of journals and to meet in New York the new generation of poets for whom she was to become a guiding spirit.

CHAPTER III ∿ OTHERS

∿ *IT IS AN EASY JOURNEY* from Chatham, New Jersey, to New York and, from 1915 on, it was a journey that Marianne Moore made increasingly often. She mentions "venturing forth to bohemian parties," [1] and one assumes that her poems in the *Egoist* and *Poetry* served as her introduction into the New York literary world. That world was young and vigorous, enthusiastic and iconoclastic. Its younger members were devoted to experimentation in literature and, because they could not readily find publishers for their work, they often undertook to publish their own literary journals. One of the most interesting of these new journals was a magazine brought out in July, 1915 by Alfred Kreymborg and Walter Arensberg. It was called *Others*, the title a reference to the fact that the editors decided there should be a more experimental alternative to Harriet Monroe's *Poetry*. The first issue included poems by William Carlos Williams, Wallace Stevens, Ezra Pound, Mina Loy, and Orrick Johns among others and caused an immediate reaction. The praise was overwhelming on the one hand, the criticism violent on the other. The editors and contributors were delighted.

That summer the *Others* group gathered frequently for Sunday picnics at Kreymborg's "shack" in Grantwood, New Jersey. Williams, according to Kreymborg, was a sort of Don Quixote figure, arriving wild and talkative in his rattletrap car. Stevens never came to the country, but Arensberg did, once bringing along Marcel Duchamp. Mary Carolyn Davies, an Oregonian who worked in a settlement house on the southwest side of New York, came frequently to Grantwood, and occasionally brought along Marianne Moore. Kreymborg remembers Miss Moore as an "astonishing person with Titian hair, a brilliant complexion and a mellifluous flow of polysyllables which held every man in awe." She "talked as she wrote and wrote as she talked, and the consummate ease of the performance either way reminded one of the rapids of an intelligent stream." [2]

They brought bundles of lunch with them and sat on the grass those Sunday afternoons discussing their work. Sometimes one or another brought a poem which, with great embarrassment, he slipped to Kreymborg for publication in *Others*. They tried reading their work aloud, but were too shy to make a success of it. Sometimes Kreymborg read it aloud for them, trying to suit his reading to their style, and this succeeded better. But mostly they talked about writing, delighted in the companionship of fellow writers.

By 1916, Miss Moore was publishing her poetry regularly in *Others* and was included in the *Others* anthology of new verse for 1916. John Marshall, who ran the Little Bookshop Around the Corner in New York, had at this time supplanted Arensberg as the financial backer of *Others* and wanted to publish single volumes of poetry by *Others* contributors. He planned volumes by Williams, Stevens, Kreymborg, Bodenheim, and Miss Moore, but actually published a volume by Kreymborg only. Miss Moore's first book did not appear for five more years and then was not published in this country.

In 1918, John Moore left Chatham to join the Navy as a chaplain and there seemed no reason for Miss Moore and her mother to remain there. They moved that year to a basement apartment on St. Luke's Place in Greenwich Village. The poet Genevieve Taggard lived nearby, Miss Moore recalls. A prizefighter lived next door.

For the next few years Miss Moore worked as a secretary in a private girls' school and as a tutor. And, of course, she wrote poetry. Her poems appeared regularly in *Others* as well as in a variety of little magazines. In 1921, she was offered a job at the Hudson Park branch of the New York Public Library, directly opposite her apartment. Since she had been a frequent visitor there, she felt the job would be at least congenial, and "ideal" if she could work only half a day—which she did, for $50 a month. She says she wasn't much good at it, could never find anything, but that she did enjoy doing the little reviews of new books that the library offered as a free public service. She would have enjoyed it more, she thinks, if the books assigned her had been other than "silent movie fiction."

Williams remembers her at about that time: "Marianne had two cords, cables rather, of red hair coiled around her rather small cranium when I first saw her and was straight up and down like the two-by-fours of a building under construction."[3] (Williams seems always to see her as a supporting structure. Elsewhere he calls her a "caryatid.") "She would laugh with a gesture of withdrawal after making some able assertion as if you yourself had said it and she were agreeing with you." In his *Autobiography* he calls her quite childlike and overt but adds, "Marianne was our saint—if we had one—in whom we all instinctually felt our purpose come together to form a stream. Everyone loved her."

Kreymborg seems to have admired the same things, her solidity and goodness and, above all, her felicitous speech. He remembers his delight in listening to her conversations with Maxwell Bodenheim, whose style of speech was, apparently, equally erudite and convoluted. They spoke in elaborate periodic sentences, subtly allusive and coming always to graceful conclusions just when Kreymborg felt surely the syntax would buckle.

Kreymborg tells of his one attempt to stump Miss Moore, get her out of her depth and render her speechless. He proposed to Williams that he could find a subject about which she knew nothing. He proceeded to take her to a Cubs and Giants game at the Polo Grounds. This occurred many years before Miss Moore's interest in baseball became public knowledge and Kreymborg had every reason to anticipate success.

They took the "El" train uptown, hanging onto the straps
in a crowded car one Saturday afternoon. Miss Moore was
undisturbed. Her perfectly balanced sentences flowed on
smoothly despite the jostling. She was speaking of poetry.

They arrived at the Polo Grounds and were seated. Miss
Moore continued talking with undiminished eloquence. She
scarcely glanced at the field, but continued to discuss the
technical achievements of Pound and Aldington. Kreymborg
had managed to bring Miss Moore on a day when Christy
Mathewson, certainly one of the most celebrated pitchers of
all time, was performing on the mound. Mathewson, Kreymborg says, began to wind up. Kreymborg interrupted Miss
Moore to say that the game was beginning and didn't she
want to watch. "'Yes, indeed,' she said, stopped, blushed, and
leaned forward."

The first pitch to Shorty Slagle was a strike. "Excellent,"
said Miss Moore. Kreymborg, a little surprised, asked her
whether she knew the name of the pitcher.

"'I've never seen him before,' she admitted, 'but I take it
it must be Mr. Mathewson.'"

Kreymborg says, "I could only gasp,
'Why?'"
to which she replied,
"'I've read his instructive book on the art of pitching—'"
The referee called "Strike two."
"'And it's a pleasure,' she continued imperturbably, 'to note
how unerringly his execution supports his theories—'"

Robert McAlmon wrote a *roman à clef, Post-Adolescence,*
about Greenwich Village life in the early 1920s. The characters
are easily recognized, and one of them, Martha Wullus, is
certainly intended as a portrait of Marianne Moore. McAlmon
gives, if not actual fact, at least the flavor of her personality,
and the reactions of others to her.

Particularly revealing is a conversation between Peter, who
is McAlmon, and Gusta Rolph, who is probably the poetess,
Mina Loy. They are speaking of Martha Wullus:

"She thinks anything, disapproves of little, for other people, and is a churchgoing, cerebralizing moralist who observes sabbath day strictly, herself—."

"It isn't reasonable to be as rigid as that with the kind of intellect she seems to have. There's some suppression or cowardice there."

"Possibly she isn't emotionally developed much, but still there's the force of experience back of her knowledge. . . . She needs to be seen apart from the background of her mother to be actual though."[4]

They feel that she is a puzzle, a quaint idea rather than a human being, as they say later. A character modelled on Marsden Hartley calls her "a Dresden doll thing with those great contemplative Chinese eyes of hers, and that wisplike body with its thatch of carrot-colored hair. So picturesque too in her half-boyish clothes."

There follows a visit to Martha Wullus and her mother. McAlmon reproduces Marianne Moore-like conversation that has about it the ring of truth. It is, as he describes it, formal, but whimsically direct. She complains gently that her work keeps her from her poetry, says that she plans to put some of her observations into verse, although this is like "trying to dance the minuet in a bathing suit." She remarks that she has things to say about seaweed, acacias and serpents in plane trees. She speaks of being unable to control her temper at the library.

I fear I spoke curtly to the head librarian for some of her trite insistences . . . But I find seahorses, lizards, and such things very fascinating. Also a fox's face, the picture of which I saw recently in a magazine, haunts me like a nightmare, and contradictory as it seems, I am quite able to appreciate the "bright beaming expression" that Xenophon talks about, on the face of the hound which was pursuing it.

Marianne Moore would have said it better, but McAlmon manages to convey the atmosphere of her mind. The restraint of her self-imposed discipline is the quality that McAlmon both stresses and is unable to understand. He finds it difficult to believe that the life she lives with her mother could be congenial. He calls it the life of an anchorite and thinks that she must wish at times to break free. Of course, these observations say as much about McAlmon as they do about Marianne Moore. The character, Martha Wullus, does not express dissatisfaction with her life; says, in fact, that if she *did* have more time she would not be prepared to write more. She says that she needs to read and to think more about certain things before she is ready to write poetry with which she, herself, will be pleased.

Living in Greenwich Village in the early 1920s, Marianne Moore was surrounded by people working, each in his own way, toward a modern statement in the arts. Besides Williams, Kreymborg, and McAlmon there were Hart Crane, Kenneth Burke, and Marsden Hartley. Wallace Stevens was a frequent visitor to the Village from his insurance office in Hartford. Conrad Aiken came often from Boston. Edna St. Vincent Millay lived in the Village in a narrow house on Bedford Street, dressing picturesquely and giving beautiful parties. Maxwell Bodenheim, Mina Loy, Lola Ridge, and E. E. Cummings all lived for longer or shorter periods nearby. The list of visitors from abroad is endless.

These artists never comprised a cohesive group in the manner of, say, Bloomsbury. Each one was pursuing an independent course. While one might cite, for example, the poets published in *Others* as forming a sort of group, Kreymborg, himself, denies it. They were all working experimentally, but the experiments took different forms.

This period was remarkable for its variety. There was no one major movement, no overriding system of thought. Instead, there were dozens of them. There was also an amazing lack of discrimination. Any or all of the dozen systems were embraced simultaneously. Science was exciting. Freud was exciting. So were Bergson and Dewey, and so was extrasensory perception, euthanasia, and the reeducating of Kansas farmers. There was room and time for everything.

Literary magazines appeared and disappeared like crocuses in spring. It was a time of experiment, a time of post-war confusion, tolerant of all sorts of artistic innovation. The artist's independence was sacred. He was entitled, expected in fact, to follow no dictates but his own. His work, sometimes quite mediocre, was celebrated simply because it was experimental.

If there were any ideas that predominated at the time, they were these two: that American culture was a morass of mediocrity whose only salvation lay in a renaissance of the arts and that a revolution in literary form was needed and much overdue. Exactly how art was to transform the American spirit was rather vague. In part it would be done through literary reviews presenting to Americans the good work being done abroad and, above all, in America. To place this concern exclusively in the twenties is misleading. Throughout the nineteenth century there had been attempts to revitalize the American spirit through an art that would be specifically American. And only a decade before the explosion of the twenties, a journal called the *Seven Arts* had been established with the stated purpose of revivifying American life through contact with the best American art.

From Sinclair Lewis to H. L. Mencken, to the expatriates Eliot and Pound, America seemed sunk in materialism. The profit motive had crushed the soul of the country, had turned America into a nation of boobs and Babbitts. It was time for America to slough off its overwhelming materialism and the emotional and imaginative sterility it bred. What was needed were American artists who could demonstrate to the nation the cultivation of the inner life.

The search for new artistic forms was linked to the repudiation of American life. Writers, particularly poets, felt that American literature was awash in sentimentality and insincerity. It was petrified in a reiteration of tired old forms. Even a writer who had something new to say was forced into insincerity by the demands of conventional poetic form and diction. Thus, a radical breaking out of these traditional forms, a discarding of standard poetic language seemed likely to lead to more honest expression. A poet not forced to find Beauty, Truth and Goodness in the same old places, not forced to express them in the same old ways, might then, in fact, have something useful to say about things of the spirit.

There was agreement about what general direction innova-

tion should take. Most important, the language of poetry
had to change, or, more precisely, the idea that there *was*
a special language suitable to poetry had to be discarded.
Any language was suitable so long as it did not rely upon
poetry's venerable clichés. New poetry demanded new metaphors unworn by generations of use. New poetry required
new form as well. If traditional meter, rhyme, and stanza
form seemed inhibiting, the poet should be free to write in
any form he chose.

Theorizing, moralizing, and ruminating in poetry were no
longer useful. If one wanted to express an idea, the idea
should be an object within the poem. Marianne Moore is a
master of this strategy, expressing an idea in a poem so that
it is as solid, as hard-edged, as any material object she describes. To give an example: her poem "Silence" observes
that deep feeling expresses itself not in silence but in restraint. This observation is as much a solid fact, a square-
edged building block in the poem, as is her image, in the
same poem, of the cat with a mouse in its mouth.

The awe in which Marianne Moore was held by her contemporaries is explainable in part, I think, by the fact that
she was already writing poetry that was highly original. Her
poems had broken with tradition. They were examples of the
sort of new poetry her contemporaries had envisioned, for
although there was agreement among poets about what innovations were required to revitalize American poetry, writing the new thing was something else.

In his autobiography, William Carlos Williams describes
Miss Moore as "like a rafter holding up the superstructure
of our uncompleted building." Kreymborg, in *Troubadour,*
speaks of his and Williams' absolute admiration for her mind.
He contrasts her with the rest of his literary associates: "What
they lacked in intellectual stability was freely and unconsciously
supplied by her." "What were we seeking?" Williams wrote in
his autobiography, "No one knew consistently enough to
formulate a 'movement.' . . . To my mind the thing that
gave us most a semblance of a cause was . . . the poetic line
and our hopes for its recovery from stodginess."

At a time when American writers were casting about uncertainly for a distinctively new mode of expression, Miss Moore, by virtue of her independent spirit, was pointing the way. For those who could understand what she had accomplished, the effect of her poetry was devastating. Williams declared that for Miss Moore destruction and creation were simultaneous. It was this combination that awed him. Not only did Miss Moore know what to discard, she knew, with a certainty that was unique, what to put in its place. The poetic line had, indeed, been recovered from stodginess. The English language had been given an acid bath so that each word shone fresh and new. This was a poetry without "poetic" diction, shorn of clichés, with a thoughtful disregard for the usual requirements of rhyme and meter. Here was something new, a genuinely new thing. And it was coming from a reticent small woman who simply wrote as she liked.

CHAPTER IV ❧ OBSERVATIONS

❧ IN 1921, MISS MOORE'S first book was published. Without her knowledge, Winifred Ellerman and Hilda Doolittle brought out the book, *Poems,* published in England by the Egoist Press. These two women, better known as Bryher and H.D., were both acquaintances of Miss Moore. Apparently, according to Miss Moore, only the two women were responsible for the collection and arrangement of the volume's twenty-four poems, all of which had appeared in magazines.

The book was a thin brocade-covered pamphlet, with the title *(Poems)* and the price (2s. 6d.) printed on paper and glued to the cover. Miss Moore is typically modest about the contents. Why anyone should dignify her "slight product" with the name poetry baffles her. Why H.D. and Bryher should have made the effort to publish the book is a mystery to her; she thought she should be allowed to be eccentric anonymously. But obviously she was pleased.

Marianne Moore's friends seemed often to be eager to take publication of her poems into their own hands. There is a letter from Williams in February of 1924 asking to publish a volume of her work. He and McAlmon proposed a book published by their Contact Press to include everything she was willing to print and to be prefaced with an essay by Williams.

A collection was published in 1924, but it came out under the imprint of the Dial Press. The book was called *Observa-*

tions; it contained all but three of the poems published in the earlier *Poems,* and added several others—all of them are comments on life, on art, and, delightfully, on some of the literary types that Miss Moore was then encountering in the Village.

The newness that Williams and Pound found in Miss Moore's work is observable in the poems in this volume. In these observations Miss Moore's wit is sharp and her comments often acerbic, as in the poem "To a Steam Roller." The poem discusses the kind of critic who is impervious to subtlety, blind to the value of new perceptions. She says, "You lack half wit. You crush all the particles down / into close conformity, and then walk back and forth on them." [1] The poem moves forward by means of a series of elaborate insults, its stolid pace and prosy matter-of-fact diction suggesting the pedestrian mind it describes.

Cousin to the Steam Roller is the "Pedantic Literalist" whose resistance to the novelties of imagination has turned his natural spontaneous heart into "a / little 'palm tree of turned wood.'" One knows this man. One has been bored by him. He is found at any party often standing next to the sort of lady described in "Those Various Scalpels." She is a female whose dress is "a magnificent square / cathedral tower of uniform / and at the same time, diverse appearance—a / species of vertical vineyard rustling in the storm / of conventional opinion." She possesses "that sophistication which is superior to opportunity." The destructive quality of this sophistication is described in every detail of her aspect: her voice "like intermingled echoes / struck from thin glasses"; her hair like "the tails of two / fighting-cocks"; her eyes, "flowers of ice and snow"; her cheeks, "these rosettes / of blood on the stone floors of French châteaux"; her hand, "a bundle of lances." She is an instrument, both fashionable and sophisticated, to be employed in the dissection of destiny. There is real power in the description of this woman. The images stand edge to bare edge like a face full of knives.

The literary young men in "Novices" who "write the sort of thing that would in their judgment interest a lady" would

not be likely to care for the power of Miss Moore's finely-
honed language. They would not, in fact, recognize it. They
are "blind to the right word, deaf to satire." They are "super-
tadpoles." They "present themselves as a contrast to sea-
serpented regions 'unlit by the half-lights of more conscious
art.'" They are, of course, ridiculous. To the fatuous babble
of their conversation Miss Moore opposes thirteen final lines
that are massive, strong, and beautiful. They speak of one of
the things that these young men, in their ignorance, disdain:
the Hebrew language. Miss Moore describes the language by
using images suggestive of the sea. Characteristically, these
lines are a network of quotations. Their arrangement produces a coherence and power that make a new thing—an
emotionally grasped sense of the majesty of the Hebrew
language.

"split like a glass against a wall"
in this "precipitate of dazzling impressions,
the spontaneous unforced passion of the Hebrew language—
an abyss of verbs full of reverberations and tempestuous energy"
in which action perpetuates action and angle is at variance with
                                                           angle
till submerged by the general action;
obscured by "fathomless suggestions of color,"
by incessantly panting lines of green, white with concussion,
in this drama of water against rocks—this "ocean of hurrying
                                                    consonants"
with its "great livid stains like long slabs of green marble,"
its "flashing lances of perpendicular lightning" and "molten
                                          fires swallowed up,"
"with foam on its barriers,"
"crashing itself out in one long hiss of spray."

   Miss Moore has said, when questioned about the extensive
use of quotations in her poems, that if a thing has been said
in the best way, it cannot be said better. "If I wanted to say
something and somebody had said it ideally, then I'd take
it but give the person credit for it. That's all there is to it."
   The Notes to the poems provided by Miss Moore serve
mainly to acknowledge the sources of the quotations used in

the poetry. These sources range all the way from newspaper advertisements to Xenophon and include the *London Illustrated News,* Francis Bacon, Ecclesiasticus, Cardinal Newman, Pliny, Duns Scotus, and the U.S. Department of Agriculture. In most cases the notes are not particularly helpful to an understanding of the poems, but are in themselves interesting as an indication of the breadth of Marianne Moore's reading and the kind of information that interests her. Her self-conscious scrupulosity has struck at least some of her readers as comical.

"Words are constructive / when they are true; the opaque allusion—the simulated / flight / upward—accomplishes nothing." So she says in the original version of "Picking and Choosing." A new thing can be constructed with the right words. Opposed to the opaque allusion is the one that transmits light to the understanding. This clarity of expression is the "white light that is the background of all good work."[2] The exactly right word, the allusion that enlightens, are the things to be sought for in the creation of poetry and in the writing of criticism. But there is also the matter of personal preference, the informing spirit of the writer in his work. In "Picking and Choosing," Miss Moore cites as good critics Gordon Craig and Kenneth Burke, men whose predilections enrich their precision of expression. To these men she opposes the critics too foolish even to know what they don't know. They are like the student ludicrously mistranslating Caesar. They are *"humming-bugs"*—wonderful sandwich of a word— who mistake a candle for an electric light and almost surely will be burned. Miss Moore asks only for a little gusto and some hard thought.

There is another sort of critic who will understand and overexplain to the point of suffocation. In "Nothing Will Cure the Sick Lion but to Eat an Ape," Miss Moore seems to be talking about him. The poem is one long sentence arranged in two stanzas. It is saved from breathlessness by the slowing effect of long words, which at the same time suggest the prose style of the overexplainer.

Even in these small early poems one can begin to see reasons for the enthusiasm that Williams and Pound expressed.

They are slight pieces compared to others in the book, but they demonstrate the precision, the economy of word and image that is characteristic of the other poems. "To a Steam Roller" is a poem of thirteen lines from which a definite personality emerges, not because the personality is easy to characterize but because each word has been chosen for its power to convey meaning.

"Those Various Scalpels" is an even better illustration of the constructive potential of the precisely chosen word, the power of the translucent image. The first four stanzas of the poem present a perfectly realized personality without a single direct statement made about character. The images used to describe the woman's external appearance speak equally for her character. The sorcery lies in the imagination that can see the hidden in the obvious, or, as Miss Moore says elsewhere, "the power of the visible / is the invisible."

Something like this idea informs the lovely long poem, "People's Surroundings." "They answer one's questions," the poem begins. That is, the external does not, as people sometimes hope, conceal the internal, but rather exemplifies it. A variety of surroundings is described. The inhabitants of the places are absent. Yet in each case, description of external detail gives us the sense of their presence.

In this, as in many of Miss Moore's poems, one becomes quickly lost in a delight of particulars. The meaning is there, certainly. The images cohere to a central core, but one wishes to stop and roll a word or two about on the tongue, to re-read a metaphor slowly, exactly as one would admire a perfect leaf, oblivious to the tree from which it had fallen. From this poem, for instance, remark the lines: "and life is like a lemon leaf" or "and turquoise blues refute the clock" or "its mockingbirds, fringed lilies and hibiscus, / its black butterflies with blue half circles on their wings, / tan goats with onyx ears" or "pierced turquoise of the lattices / and the acacia-like lady shivering. . . ." There is a real pleasure here in Miss Moore's artistry, unconnected with any concern for her content. Miss Moore's poetry is a feast of such particular pleasures.

She has sometimes been called an Imagist in the past, although she disclaims any connection to the Imagist movement. Perhaps the association has been made because of her friendship with many of the poets who at one time or another professed to be writing Imagist poetry. Another and more likely reason is the recognition of her concern for the precise image to convey a perception. Some of the images that I have just quoted might, out of context, seem to substantiate the claim. They are, after all, meant to describe precisely an impression. However, the images taken within the poem have a significance which reaches further than the object's boundaries. They comment at the same time that they describe.

Eliot, in his 1935 Introduction to Miss Moore's *Selected Poems,* says that so far back as his memory extends, "Miss Moore has no immediate poetic derivations." He cites "A Talisman" from *Observations* as a poem that is perhaps slightly influenced by H.D.'s brand of Imagism. "But," he says, "even here the cadence, the use of rhyme, and a certain authoritativeness of manner distinguish the poem."

"The aim of 'imagism,'" Eliot says, "so far as I understand it, or so far as it had any, was to induce a peculiar concentration upon something visual, and to set in motion an expanding succession of concentric feelings." He says that Miss Moore's poems, particularly those with animal or bird subjects, while seeming to concentrate on a particular object, actually have a very wide spread of association.

Stanley Coffman, in his book *Imagism,* discusses those aspects of Marianne Moore's poetry that might be considered Imagistic: the exactness of detail, clarity of impression, concern for making the object real even though it exists in an imagined context. He makes this distinction: "She chooses to write about an object, however, because she finds in it certain characteristics whose significance extends beyond the object." [3]

The confusion of Miss Moore with the Imagists, insofar as it has existed, has been a matter of seeing in similarities of technique an identity of purpose. Marianne Moore has used exactness, concentration upon and detailed description of a particular object in the service of idea and emotion. As Eliot says in his Introduction, "For a mind of such agility, and for a sensibility so reticent, the minor subject . . . may be the best release for the major emotions."

Nonetheless, between 1914 and 1920 Marianne Moore had been writing poems in harmony with new theories of modern poetry. Apparently quite independently, she was writing the sort of poetry that Pound and others were saying ought to be written. Use of the exact word and the language of ordinary speech, new and freer rhythms that would accommodate themselves to the content rather than demand accommodation, clarity, and concentration of expression, and the particular image in place of the abstract generalization—all of these innovations were being practiced by Miss Moore as they were being preached by Pound.

Eliot, in his Introduction, says of Miss Moore, "I should say that she had taken to heart the repeated reminder of Mr. Pound: that poetry should be as well written as prose. She seems to have saturated her mind in the perfections of prose, in its precision rather than its purple; and to have found her rhythm, her poetry, her appreciation of the individual word, for herself."

The flavor of prose brought to spare perfection is certainly evident in "Critics and Connoisseurs." The poem is composed of clear declarative sentences, and ends with an interrogative. One has the impression of words having been selected and placed by tweezers in their context. The poem begins, "There is a great amount of poetry in unconscious / fastidiousness." There is a great amount of fastidiousness—conscious or unconscious—in this poem. Note, for example, the lines, "Certain Ming / products, imperial floor-coverings of coach- / wheel yellow, are well enough in their way but I have seen something / that I like better. . . ." Or later, a swan of whom it is said: "Finally its hardihood was / not proof against its / proclivity to more fully appraise such bits / of food as the stream / bore counter to it." These lines might be found in an essay. There is nothing specifically poetic about them and, yet, they are superb poetry. Expression is shaved to essentials here. The words used defy substitution. They are crystals of accuracy. Yet the music of the lines spools down the page like silk thread and the poem, so determinedly matter-of-fact, contains such an image as this: "I remember a swan under the willows in Oxford, / with flamingo-coloured, maple- / leaflike feet."

This poem speaks of those critics and connoisseurs who attach importance to attitudes and goals that have no purpose beyond themselves. They are like the swan whose attitudinizing almost prevents his unbending enough to eat the food that is offered him. They are like the ant struggling to carry a useless piece of whitewash on a pointless errand. This is conscious fastidiousness, a rigidity which, as Sir Herbert Read has suggested in speaking of this poem, is proof against the impact of random experience and the promptings of the unconscious.[4] Miss Moore asks the purpose of such rigidity. It is a hampering attitude for a critic, she seems to say, and by extension, one might conclude, an almost fatal attitude for a poet.

Miss Moore prefers the natural to the artificial, innocent honesty to sophisticated obfuscation. When she writes of the various literary people in the poems in *Observations*, it is the artificial pose, the deadening intellection and sophistication that she criticizes. "Truth is no Apollo / Belvedere, no formal thing" she says in "In The Days of Prismatic Color." Truth is the plain and clear and simple. It is the honesty of pure color, the lucidity of clear air. She says,

> Complexity,
> moreover, that has been committed to darkness, instead of
>
> granting itself to be the pestilence that it is, moves all a-
> bout as if to bewilder us with the dismal
> fallacy that insistence
> is the measure of achievement and that all
> truth must be dark. Principally throat, sophistication is as it al-
>
> ways has been—at the antipodes from the init-
> ial great truths.

Pound would approve that statement. The preference for clarity here is more than a matter of taste. It is an ethic. Deliberate obfuscation is a species of immorality. The use of murky, equivocal expression in literature is evidence of a dishonest mind. This equating of style with moral integrity is a peculiarly modern idea. As a man's character might once have been read in his face, so now it could be found in his mode of expression. Honesty of intention would lead a man to be as accurate in his choice of words and as clear in his syntax as possible. The new emphasis on precision, particularity, and clarity, then, was as much a moral stand as it was a stylistic rebellion.

In her well-known poem, "Poetry," Miss Moore begins, "I too, dislike it." This line has been interpreted as ironic, as an attempt to disarm, or as evidence that she practices her art only half-seriously. Quite obviously, however, her reasoning is serious. She refers to a kind of poetry that is neither honest nor sincere but that has found fashionable approval by virtue of its very obscurity.

"Poetry" has had several incarnations. The last version, appearing in the *Complete Poems* of 1967, is four lines long, having been cut from a poem of thirty-eight lines that appeared in the *Selected Poems* of 1935 and the *Collected Poems* of 1951. This longer version, in turn, grew out of the original thirteen lines printed in *Observations*. The last revision was, I think, a mistake. For one thing, the poem of four lines is so brief that it invites misinterpretation. The words "dislike" and "contempt" overshadow the idea that poetry has also a place for the genuine and, without knowing the earlier versions, a reader might very well feel confused. What poetry is she referring to? All poetry? Some particular kind? It isn't clear in the short version. In this case the concision itself results in a kind of obscurity.

The middle version is the one I like best. The thirteen lines in *Observations* are thin by comparison to the longer poem of 1935. The *Observations* version makes clear that Miss Moore is denigrating a particular kind of modern poetry in which intellectualization has led to incomprehensibility, but it does not, as the longer version does, seek to define what poetry ought to be. The longer 1935 version does this. It defines poems using Miss Moore's well-known phrase " 'imaginary gardens with real toads in them' " and poets as " 'literalists of the imagination.' " Imagination is placed in opposition to intellection. The raw material for poetry abounds, it is everywhere, is anything, but it must be imaginatively grasped.

Imagination proceeds from a deeper source than intellection. When, in "Melanchthon," Miss Moore speaks of the "beautiful element of unreason" underlying the poet's tough outer hide, I think she is talking about the place where imagination grows. The "element" is genuine because it cannot be otherwise, its source mysterious, hidden under layers of the rational mind. Poetry, then, when it is genuine, is a collision of this private vision with the outside world. It is an imaginary garden full of real toads. This is thought that needs emphasis; I miss it in the four-line poem.

Perhaps Miss Moore felt that she was following her own advice on compression. One is reminded of the words " 'compression is the first grace of style' " that Miss Moore quotes from Democritus in her poem, "To a Snail." "Contractility is a virtue" she says. What we find valuable in style is "the principle that is hid." The snail, because of its particular physical attributes, has its own " 'method of conclusions,' " its own " 'knowledge of principles' " just as the individual poet has a style determined by his own particularities, determined especially by the hidden principle of his imagination. But in the final version of "Poetry" the virtue of compression has been carried too far. The hidden principle has been too well hidden.

I prefer among Miss Moore's poems the ones which most clearly "acknowledge the spiritual forces which have made [them]" as she has said speaking of her own preferences in "When I Buy Pictures." Certainly the use of prose-like statement, the matter-of-fact expression of belief, is a part of her style that is wholly personal. But it seems to me that the spiritual forces are best displayed when these prosy bits serve to frame her astonishing images. In "Poetry," last version, the images have been sacrificed. A poem like "A Grave" seems to me more satisfying because of the combination of prose and image, statement and mystery. The poem is truly " 'lit with piercing glances into the life of things,' " to quote again from "When I Buy Pictures."

"A Grave" is a poem describing the sea, but it is naming a particular sea that exists as much in the poet's imagination as in the outside world. It is not an ocean with green islands and sunlight, not an ocean with sailboats and whitecaps, not even a sea of storms and breakers. It is an ocean full of human bones. One can imagine the ocean in a number of guises; to choose to see it as a dangerous and malignant force is to say as much about oneself as about the sea.

The emotional charge of the poem is in excess of what one might reasonably expect from the ostensible content. People drown in the ocean, of course, an unlucky few, but certainly it is overstatement to say "the sea has nothing to give but a well excavated grave." In the work of a poet of such typical reticence and restraint, overstatement bears investigation. One begins to look for "the principle that is hid."

the sea is a collector, quick to return a rapacious look.
There are others besides you who have worn that look—
whose expression is no longer a protest; the fish no longer
                                        investigate them
for their bones have not lasted:
men lower nets, unconscious of the fact that they are
                                        desecrating a grave,
and row quickly away—the blades of the oars
moving together like the feet of water spiders as if there were
                                        no such thing as death.

The sinister images contained in these lines have the quality of nightmare, the emotional supercharge of the dream image. There are other places a man may drown. Life itself can be a malignant element. One can feel danger living in an indifferent universe. One can feel danger when one lowers a net into the unconscious mind, that grave of bones with its flotsam of old memory and fear.

This fearsome and chaotic element, whatever its name, is the major reality. In opposition one may erect a grid of order: "The firs stand in a procession, each with an emerald turkey / foot at the top, / reserved as their contours, saying nothing." One may provide lighthouses, bell-buoys. One may choose to see the water "beautiful under networks of foam." But the sea dominates. It is not ignored nor controlled nor made safe by these things. It "advances as usual, looking as if it were not that ocean in which / dropped things are bound to sink— / in which if they turn and twist, it is neither with volition nor consciousness."

This is imagination transforming reality with total mastery. Unobtrusively anthropomorphic, the language used creates a sea that exists mysteriously in the emotions. One thinks of the ocean imagery used to describe the Hebrew language in "Novices." In both cases the power and mystery of this deepest of waters finds a parallel in that which is deepest in man.

"An Octopus" is Marianne Moore exuberantly herself in another way. Again, one is conscious everywhere of a particular imagination at work stamping each line with a familiar monogram. This long poem, as Miss Moore's appended notes make clear, is a collection of facts about mountains and animals and plants culled and quoted from sources as various as the *Illustrated London News,* U.S. Government pamphlets about national parks, and words overheard at a circus. The whole is taken together as a description of "Big Snow Mountain" replete with a dozen sorts of mountain animals and catalogs of mountain flowers, included, one senses, out of pure relish for their names. Catalogs of irresistible names and compilations of quotations are typical in Miss Moore's poetry. They are the real toads she sets artistically in her imaginary gardens.

Few people would think to describe a mountain as looking like an octopus with "pseudopodia." Fewer still would be likely to call the needles of the larch tree "polite," or a waterfall "an endless skein swayed by the wind." Nobody but Miss Moore would write "miniature cavalcades of chlorophylless fungi." These sorts of observations, as individual as thumb prints, together with dozens of quoted lines, construct an imaginary mountain, fanciful and complex. The mountain has all the complexity of life itself. Like life it is jagged and, in its variety, mysterious. It has an existence that defies man's attempts to explain and interpret.

The Greeks liked smoothness, distrusting what was back
of what could not be clearly seen,
resolving with benevolent conclusiveness,
"complexities which still will be complexities
as long as the world lasts";

They were, Miss Moore says, "'like happy souls in Hell,'" ignoring, one gathers, what they did not wish to acknowledge. Miss Moore has little patience with this fondness for surfaces. Life cannot be reduced to simplified equations. Ignoring its snagged complexity is a kind of refusal of life itself.

Henry James, she says, was

"damned by the public for decorum";
not decorum, but restraint;
it is the love of doing hard things
that rebuffed and wore them out—

One hard thing to do is willingly to embrace the mysteries and contradictions of existence, to permit variety and uncertainty, to have, like James, like the mountain, a capacity for fact.

It interests me that the central image of this poem should be an octopus. Nothing is random, particularly in the poetry of Marianne Moore. When a mountain notable for its complexity is compared to an ocean animal "beneath a sea of shifting snow dunes," I find it irresistible to connect the image to other sea imagery encountered. Increasingly the sea seems to function in the poetry as an analogue for the unconscious. An animal from this source, an octopus whose nature is "relentless accuracy" and a "capacity for fact" might, then, be also a poem, its source the imagination and its raw material, fact. The octopus that is the mountain is the poem.

Perhaps poetry *is* the subject of all poetry, as critics have said. At any rate, frequently a poem can be read that way without putting undue strain on the imagery. "Sea Unicorns and Land Unicorns" is an example. The unicorns and lions found on old maps and tapestries are the poem's ostensible subjects; "sea lions and land lions, / land unicorns and sea unicorns . . . / this fourfold combination of strange animals, / upon embroideries. . . . Thus personalities by nature much opposed / can be combined in such a way / that when they do agree, their unanimity is great."

Well, what better metaphor for poetry is there than this combination of imaginative beast and real one, land animal and animal from the sea? When the intellect combines with feeling, the imagination with reality, the coherence is poetry.

The unicorns of the poem are spoken of as real animals. The unicorn is miraculously elusive, " 'impossible to take alive.' " And yet it can be tamed by "a lady inoffensive like itself— / as curiously wild and gentle." Imagination cannot be forced or trapped. To try to bring it to the ground is to kill it, but it can perhaps be induced by an openness of mind in which fancy and feeling are given unlimited license.

Fancy and feeling. These two, together with observation of the outside world, are the material of Miss Moore's poetry. One is reminded of the frequent charge that Miss Moore's poetry lacks feeling, that it is precise but frigid work. As T. S. Eliot said in the Introduction I have quoted so often, "feeling in one's own way, however intensely, is likely to look like frigidity to those who can only feel in accepted ways."

Miss Moore's remark that "the deepest feeling always shows itself in silence; / not in silence, but restraint" is a clue to reading the poetry. These feelings are not silenced but they are held in restraint by such formal means as precision of diction and choice of subject. In later poems she is everywhere expressing feeling, but it wears the disguise of exotic animals or is hidden at the center of the driest metaphysical comment. Further, Miss Moore's desire for accuracy prevents her using language that has become the ordinary vocabulary of emotion. The trigger words that one has come to expect in description of feeling are missing. Always the feeling is restrained, expressed with qualifications and unsparing accuracy, and in such guise that it may not be apparent to those who wish to be disarmed by easy emotion.

To express oneself with restraint is not necessarily to be bound by repression. A preference for precision rather than effusion may be a matter of taste. When, in "Silence," Miss Moore tells us that " 'make my house your inn' " is not an evidence of unrestraint since "inns are not residences," she is both praising and embodying precision. As when describing visual images she seeks words that will exactly express the quality of the thing, so, too, in the case of feeling. Eschewing the easy words for the ambiguous emotion is a species of honesty and not evidence of lack of depth.

One formal kind of restraint a poet places upon himself and his expression, of course, is his versification. Even in the sort of modernist poetry Miss Moore was writing in *Observations,* the versification is not "free." She employs formal patterns of complicated syllabic lines. Often the poems are unrhymed, others are rhymed irregularly. Rhyme may occur regularly in the middle of lines that have unrhymed endings. Frequently, a rhyme pattern is used which exists separately or in contrast to the rhythmic pattern. That is, the rhymes fall not where the stress would lead one to expect them, not even, indeed, where the sense of the lines might dictate rhyme, but in a pattern laid like lace over the top of these stronger impulses. Eliot calls this "light rhyme" and says that Miss Moore is its greatest living master.

The exigencies of syllabics and the use of light rhyme can result in poems that both look and sound eccentric. The syllabic count in a poem, for instance, frequently requires peculiar enjambement—lines that end with a preposition or an article, or idiosyncratic hyphenation as in the word "bal- / lasted." Light rhyme, too, results in unorthodox uses. In the poem, "The Fish," articles are occasionally used as rhyme words: "an / injured fan"; "the / turquoise sea." Unusual placement of emphasis is required: "All / external"; and totally arbitrary hyphenation occurs: "ac- / cident—lack."

Often, as in "The Fish," the title of the poem is also its opening line. This has been done, we are told, to spare our having to read the same thing twice. In "The Fish," however, these words are not included as part of the poem so far as the syllabic count is concerned.

I find these eccentricities of versification charming. It is as though a private joke were being offered to the reader who took the trouble to study the poem's construction. At no time do I feel Miss Moore's presence more closely than when I am noticing the means she has taken to preserve her syllable count.

"The Fish" is one of my favorites among all the poems. It has the appealing eccentricities of versification already mentioned and it has some of the loveliest images in all of the poetry: "The Fish / wade / through black jade. / Of the crow-blue mussel-shells, one keeps / adjusting the ash heaps; / opening and shutting itself like / an / injured fan," and "submerged shafts of the / sun, / split like spun / glass," and "crabs like green / lilies, and submarine / toadstools, slide each on the other." In addition, there is the mystery of emotion and sense of hidden content that informs others of Miss Moore's most affecting poems. I do not fully understand this poem. The last lines, "the chasm side is / dead. / Repeated / evidence has proved that it can live / on what cannot revive / its youth. The sea grows old in it" are moving without being entirely penetrable.

The subject, again, is a sea that is powerful in its potential for injury. The mussel shell is like an injured fan. The barnacles cannot hide. The water has driven a wedge of iron through the cliff. The cliff itself is scarred, both by the sea and by other forces. It is defiant but its chasm side is dead. The defiance of the cliff is echoed in the theme of armored endurance encountered in numbers of the later poems. Defiance is a kind of persevering. Endurance, in itself a species of restraint, is the only armoring possible, Miss Moore seems to be saying.

The fusion of content and rhythm in this poem is remarkable. The theme of endurance is echoed in the restraint of the line. By no means may the lines be read so that they flow smoothly. The arbitrary requirements of the syllabic pattern produce odd pauses in the flow of meaning between lines so that there is a sense of repeated blockage. The rhythm is halting as though pent and straining against an obstacle. Words are used in such a way that they must be pronounced precisely and singly as, for example, "Sun / split like spun / glass." The effect is a staccato pattern within the straining line. Reading the poem aloud, one has an almost physical sense of being held back, forced into control by the exigencies of the poem's structure.

The version of "The Fish" appearing in the *Collected Poems* was changed from the earlier version in *Observations,* a five-line stanza being substituted for the earlier poem's six-line one. The alteration was made by removing a one-syllable line that occurred as the fourth line of each stanza and adding it to the end of the third line. The result is greater elegance. The sense of staccato movement is not diminished, but is made more subtle by this change; and the appearance of the printed poem is more graceful.

Eliot speaks of "a precise fitness of form and matter . . . a balance between them." "The Fish" is an outstanding instance of fitness, but there are many others. In the poem "England," long lines and long words are a suitable vehicle for ruminations. Miss Moore is here defending to its detractors America in all its naïve homeliness. It is

the wild man's land; grassless, linksless, languageless country in
                                   which letters are written
not in Spanish, not in Greek, not in Latin, not in shorthand,
but in plain American which cats and dogs can read!

One should not imagine that because America lacks polish and sophistication it lacks substance as well. Of superiority, Miss Moore concludes, "It has never been confined to one locality." The poem is a meditation and defense and the long prosy line with its essayistic words (criterion, misapprehension, discernment, sublimated) seems entirely proper.

Proper, too, is the shorter, energetic line of "Sojourn in the Whale." The rhythms, progressing through a series of restless clauses, seem impatient, as if reflecting the dominant feeling of the poem. Miss Moore is impatient with the condescension of the English to Ireland. This sojourn in the British whale may be temporary, Ireland may rise against its captivity, but the belittling attitude of the English is annoying nonetheless. Ireland is characterized as female in this poem so that one wonders parenthetically whether some suggestion of the repression of women in a man's world may have been intended as well. Certainly the patronizing attitude expressed in the lines, "There is a feminine temperament in direct contrast to ours / which makes her do these things," must have had parallels in the experience of a woman working in the essentially male world of literature in 1924.

In 1923, the poem "Marriage" was published in Monroe Wheeler's little pamphlet series, *Manikin,* then reprinted in 1924 in *Observations.* It is one of Miss Moore's most difficult poems. It is long, consisting of some 280 short lines, ordinarily six to eight syllables in length. The meaning, in places, is nearly impenetrable. Part of the difficulty of the poem arises, I think, from its structure.

William Carlos Williams, in his essay, "Marianne Moore," says: "The only help I ever got from Miss Moore toward the understanding of her verse was that she despised connectives."[5] He says that one may search at length in the exciting mazes of her poetry, sure that he will eventually discover the right door. The poem will finally be discovered to be complete and fully comprehensible. One will find that only the connectives are missing.

This absence of connectives is, I think, one of the primary sources of difficulty in "Marriage." The transition from idea to idea and image to image is made without the help of explanatory language. It is assumed that the relationships between ideas or the link between images will be grasped, not because they are verbally conjoined, but because they have essential connection.

This method, which expects the imagination of the reader to make the necessary link, is as rewarding as it is demanding. It requires an action like that demanded by a metaphor. When a poet speaks of cherry lips, the link is easily seen. When a poet speaks of a mountain as an octopus of ice, it takes the reader more effort to see the connection essentially joining these things. But when the connection *is* imaginatively understood, the effect of the less obvious metaphor will be more powerful.

Williams called "Marriage" "an anthology of transit" because of its method of swift, verbally unconnected transition from thought to thought. The effort required of the reader to follow the sense of the poem through these transitions accounts in part for the poem's effectiveness. Loss of focus does not occur because nothing is held too long in focus. As one cannot look too long at a picture without beginning not to see it, so one cannot dwell too long on an idea without its beginning to lose its first power. If one looks away from the picture and then looks back, vision is refreshed and reintensified. Painters have sought to eliminate this fuzzing of attention by means of distortion or abstraction: if a greater effort of imagination is required to recognize a pear or an apple in geometric abstraction, then the attention is automatically increased. Similarly, the speed of transition and the lack of verbal connection in "Marriage" engage the imagination of the reader to such a degree that every few lines produces a shock of reintensified understanding. Another way of saying somewhat the same thing is this explanation that Williams gives of good modern poetry. "It is a multiplication of impulses that by their several flights, crossing at all eccentric angles, might enlighten." This is the method of "Marriage." The poem is a mixture of dialogue and speculation, witty and paradoxical, sometimes serious, impelled by a tempo that leaps from point to point like an astronaut leaping at one-sixth gravity.

The poem begins with an ironic comment on the institution "perhaps one should say enterprise" itself, its essentially private nature and its thoroughly public manifestation. Miss Moore wonders how modern marriage would seem to Adam and Eve. She posits a modern Eve, beautiful, accomplished, and demanding. As Eve was the central flaw in the "first crystal-fine experiment" that was Eden, so modern woman in her independence is often considered the central flaw in the ordinary marriage. Marriage, like Eden, is "this amalgamation which can never be more / than an interesting impossibility," human independence and curiosity being what they are. As long as the institution involves bondage, it will, for people of certain temperaments, not succeed. As Eve was blamed for eating the apple, "that invaluable accident / exonerating Adam," so modern woman bears criticism for her wish for independence.

Adam, too, is beautiful, and he is a sage and a prophet. He takes himself rather too seriously though: " 'he experiences a solemn joy / in seeing that he has become an idol,' " and he forgets that there is an independent quality of mind in woman that in marriage makes his pontificating unsafe.

He is plagued by the nightingale, by "not its silence, but its silences." There follows a quotation from Edward Thomas's *Feminine Influence on the Poets* concerning the frustration of trying to induce that state of imaginative intuition which he regards as essentially feminine. The nightingale's fitful song, the imagination's intermittent flashes, unnerve Adam. Even here, in his own mind, he cannot control the independent female principle—a fact which irritates him.

In this state of frustration, Adam "stumbles over marriage, / 'a very trivial object indeed' " that for all its triviality can present formidable challenges. Friction is inevitable and is not a calamity for " 'no truth can be fully known / until it has been tried / by the tooth of disputation.' " There follow several lines I simply do not understand, ending with the ironic remark that the special hand of affection that squeezes one to the bone does not intend by this a species of bondage.

" 'But at five o'clock / the ladies in their imperious humility / are ready to receive you,' " showing that "men have power / and sometimes one is made to feel it." Both man and woman, then, reserve to themselves the right of independence. Men are more blatant in their assertion, but women in their paradoxically "imperious humility" make assertions of their own.

A dialogue between this modern Adam and Eve follows, each expressing unflattering opinions of the other. They love themselves too much, Miss Moore suggests, to permit them to love each other and "one is not rich but poor / when one can always seem so right."

A marriage of independence within union is rare but still to be desired. It would be "that striking grasp of opposites / opposed each to the other, not to unity," "that charitive Euroclydon / of frightening disinterestedness." Miss Moore quotes Daniel Webster speaking of the state, " 'Liberty and union / now and forever,' " and ends the poem by suggesting an old tintype wedding picture in the lines, "the Book on the writing table; / the hand in the breast-pocket."

There are lovely flights of lyricism in this poem. I find particularly affecting these lines:

> Below the incandescent stars
> below the incandescent fruit,
> the strange experience of beauty;
> its existence is too much;
> it tears one to pieces
> and each fresh wave of consciousness
> is poison.

But there are others, as when marriage is described as "this fire-gilt steel / alive with goldenness," as in the lines:

> in that Persian miniature of emerald mines
> raw silk—ivory white, snow white,
> oyster white, and six others—
> that paddock full of leopards and giraffes—
> long lemon-yellow bodies
> sown with trapezoids of blue.

or:

> The blue panther with black eyes,
> the basalt panther with blue eyes,
> entirely graceful—
> one must give them the path—
> the black obsidian Diana

who 'darkeneth her countenance
as a bear doth.'

These last two passages happen, as well, to be the most impenetrable in the poem. I have tried to decide whether their very obscurity in some sense explains their beauty, whether because the meaning is unclear the words themselves command disproportionate attention. I think, rather, that both passages are evidence of an intensity of imagination and a concentration of feeling so private that, although the meaning is hidden, the quality of emotion remains. They are like music in their resistance to paraphrase and like music, too, in their weight of ineluctable feeling.

One can say of Miss Moore's poetry what she has said of Pound: "To cite passages is to pull one quill from a porcupine."[6] To choose from *Observations* poems for attention becomes finally an arbitrary matter. I have here looked at most of the poems that are widely praised as the great ones, and I have included others that please me especially; but *Observations* is full of poems no less good. "New York," for instance, calls the place "the savage's romance" and contains such satisfying lines as "wilting eagles' down compacted by the wind" and "to the conjunction of the Monongahela and the Allegheny." One of "the labors of Hercules," in a poem of the same name, is "to popularize the mule, its neat exterior / expressing the principle of accommodation reduced to a minimum." This talent for precision, this commerce in matter-of-fact statement made poetic by the very bare-boned, chiselled accuracy, is everywhere in the poetry. One learns in "Snakes, Mongooses, Snake Charmers, and the Like" that "The passion for setting people right is in itself an afflictive disease. / Distaste which takes no credit to itself is best." In "To Statecraft Embalmed" there are the lines "As if a death mask ever could replace / life's faulty excellence!" and "Discreet behavior is not now the sum / of statesmanlike good sense."

Of the fifty-three poems in *Observations,* forty-four reappear in one or more of Miss Moore's later volumes. Among the poems left out of later collections, "Dock Rats" is, perhaps, the only questionable omission. It has life and charm and flavor and, while not as fine nor as imaginative as the best poems, it seems salvageable for the felicities it does contain. Of the other omissions, all seem wise. "Radical" is clumsy by comparison to other poems in the volume. "Talisman," the poem that Eliot in his Introduction to the *Selected Poems* likened to the style of H.D., is also criticized by him for its commonplace sentiment and the inaccuracy of its description. "Reticence and Volubility," "To an Intra-Mural Rat" and "Reinforcements" are, each in their own way, more uncertain and amateurish than other poems in the book.

Many of the poems that reappear later have undergone extensive revision. It is interesting to study the revisions: they demonstrate clearly Miss Moore's tendency to greater and greater concision. The radical cutting of "Poetry" from the original version to the version appearing in the *Complete Poems* is an instance of this. The poem, "Peter," is another and, I think, more successful example of revision in the service of increased precision. The poem appeared originally in *Observations* and again in the *Collected Poems* in seven five-line stanzas. In the *Complete Poems* it is one long, unbroken stanza. There is a shift from the use of the possessive pronoun to the definite article and a progressive economizing of words: "on his foreleg which corresponds" becomes: "on *the* foreleg, which corresponds" and, finally, is changed to the shorter, less particular, "on the foreleg corresponding." The line "as it were a piece of seaweed tamed and weakened by / exposure to the sun" becomes less awkward, more elegant as revised: "as seaweed is tamed and weakened by the sun."

In her later poems and in the revisions, Miss Moore comments less on what is obvious, or nearly so, in the context of the poem. Thus, the lines:

—Demonstrate on him how
the lady caught the dangerous southern snake, placing a forked
    stick on either
side of its innocuous neck.

become in the *Complete Poems:*

Demonstrate on him how the lady placed a forked stick on the
innocuous neck-sides of the dangerous southern snake.

She has avoided the word "caught," which is implicit in the
action described, she has smoothed the line with the substitution of "innocuous neck-sides" for "on either side of its innocuous neck." And in the longer, unbroken lines she has
achieved greater elegance.

There are a number of other small revisions in the poem
"Peter" that, when studied, may all be recognized as contributing to added precision and to more graceful expression. Precision is in this case intended to provide both extreme accuracy
of description and exact clarification of meaning. Peter, the cat,
illustrates recognizably human traits, "that he does not regard
the published fact as a surrender," for instance. This line
originally read, "that he is one of those who do not regard /
the published fact as a surrender." The cutting of the words
"is one of those who" creates a finer subtlety of meaning,
permitting the intended parallel to remain clear while at the
same time better preserving the cat-like quality of Peter.

Few books have indexes that may be read for pleasure.
Few volumes of poetry have indexes at all. *Observations* has
one. Surely compiled by Miss Moore herself, it provides such
entries as: "orchid, greenish, 87"; "orchids, collision of, 67."
Under elephant there are noted: "elephant to ride, 22";
"elephants pushing, 30"; "fog-colored, 40." There are two
entries for beaver: "beaver, skin, 65"; "beavers, thoughtful,
84." Then there is this notation: "pulled, 20."

The whimsy of the index is a final measure of enjoyment
in a book that is full of special pleasures. Miss Moore's poetry
will be seen to broaden and deepen in later volumes. Her
technique gains in subtlety. Her hand becomes surer, her content fuller and richer. Yet *Observations* contains some of my
favorite poems. The mastery that appears in the later poetry
has all its seeds beginning to sprout in *Observations.*

Various people have reported finding influences in Miss

Moore's poetry. Pound thought he detected the influence of Laforgue and other French poets, but Miss Moore claims not to have read any of them until fairly recently. Harry Levin has found a tinge of French classicism, particularly in her use of the syllabic line.[7] Again, she denies the influence. She admits influences from prose, but what she means is that she admires certain felicitous phrases which she encounters in prose and which she often includes with full attribution in her poetry. Her style, however, owes nothing to anyone. It is her own.

Miss Moore has always insisted upon pleasing herself, working according to no standard but her own. She says in an essay, "Feeling and Precision," that "any concern about how well one's work is going to be received seems to mildew effectiveness." In another essay she praises the cartoonist, David Low, for holding to his own standards, "—he has never compromised; he goes right on doing what idiosyncrasy tells him to do. The thing is to see the vision and not deny it; to care and admit that we do."

One thinks of her in connection with Walt Whitman, that most "American" of poets. In both cases being American meant simply being self-reliant, trusting to inward vision rather than received form. Of course, this is no more American than it is Rumanian or Chinese. It is seeing the vision and not denying it. It is an acceptance of oneself.

It was the idiosyncratic vision that informed both Miss Moore's work and her character that excited Williams and baffled McAlmon. Her determination to remain true to that vision resulted in a kind of strength that could, indeed, serve as a superstructure, a caryatid for a new movement in American poetry.

CHAPTER V ⤫ THE DIAL

⤫ IN 1924, MISS MOORE received the *Dial* Award for *Observations*. The award of $2,000 was presented, as the *Dial* editors carefully stipulated, not as a prize, which would imply something competed for, but as an award given in recognition of merit, to enable the recipient to work as he wished and, thereby, to enrich and develop his art. "Nor was a gift ever more complete and without victimizing involvements,"[1] Miss Moore has said.

The *Dial*, in 1924, was without doubt the most prestigious of the literary periodicals in this country and, many would say, the world. The aim of its editors was to publish the best work available, domestic or foreign, regardless of the reputation of the author. The policy led to the publication of a great many new and experimental writers as well as those whose reputations had become established. Excellence was the only criterion and it was for this that Miss Moore was recognized.

Miss Moore had been the first poet of the *Others* group to be published in the *Dial*, with a poem appearing in 1920 Kreymborg tells of a party that Lola Ridge gave at the time that *Others* was collapsing, about 1919. The little magazine had been moribund for months, revived only sporadically when some one contributor or group of contributions managed to edit another issue. In the final days, Kreymborg says, Lola Ridge continued to try to keep the group together and the spirit of *Others* viable by giving a party nearly every time she sold an article or poem.

It was at one of these parties that Scofield Thayer, who had just taken over editorship of the *Dial*, heard Marianne Moore read her poetry. The party, in what Kreymborg describes as Lola Ridge's "dark room on Fifteenth Street," was a crowded affair. There were a number of *Others* contributors, among them Wallace Stevens, Williams, Orrick Johns, and Miss Moore. Witter Bynner was there, Waldo Frank, and Percy MacKaye. And there were newcomers with a variety of aesthetic outlooks. Late in the evening, Scofield Thayer arrived.

Thayer's arrival was of great interest to a number of these people. The first issue of the *Dial* under his editorship had not yet appeared, but rumors circulated that this was the magazine that would bring the millenium for artists in America.

As the evening progressed someone suggested reading aloud. Stevens, ordinarily reticent, finally read something, although, Kreymborg says, he "waited for conversation to reach a fairly confused height before he drew forth a paper that looked like a poem but sounded like a tête-à-tête with himself." Johns, Kreymborg, and Williams read, and finally, at about two in the morning, Marianne Moore joined them. She read "England" in a voice that, Kreymborg says, was barely audible. When she had finished Thayer apprehended her and, in whispered conversation, persuaded her to let him have the poem for the *Dial*.

Miss Moore's version of the incident is as follows: She had sent some things to the *Dial* previously which were sent back. Then, "Lola Ridge had a party . . . And much to my disgust, we were induced each to read something we had written. And Scofield Thayer said of my piece, 'Would you send that to us at the *Dial*?' "

" 'I did send it,' I said.

"And he said, 'Well, send it again.' "

The first five issues of the *Dial* in 1925 carried tributes to Miss Moore's work. In the citation that accompanied the *Dial* Award, Thayer had called her "America's most distinguished poetess,"[2] a title that he said had been vacant since the death of Emily Dickinson. Her poetry, he said, was for "the informed literary middle-of-the-road" combining "the rewards of experiment with the comforts of custom." Now Glenway Wescott continued the praise in the January issue, calling Miss Moore's poetry "an object lesson in the exploitation of an environment by a mind." In February, March, and April there was praise of Miss Moore in the unsigned column called "Comments." In May, Williams reviewed *Observations* for the magazine. In June, the *Dial* announced that Miss Moore would become acting editor beginning with the July, 1925, issue upon the resignation of Scofield Thayer. Thus Miss Moore assumed what William Wasserstrom, in his book *The Time of the Dial*, has called "the most influential literary post in New York."

The *Dial* was a periodical with a distinguished past. The name had first been used by Ralph Waldo Emerson and Margaret Fuller for a critical magazine published in Cambridge, Massachusetts in 1840. In the best tradition of the critical little magazine, this one perished in 1844, as a result of financial distress. In 1880, the name was revived for a critical magazine published in Chicago by Francis F. Browne. It survived as a sort of academic monthly until 1916, when Martyn Johnson became owner, appointed George Bernard Donlin editor and assembled a group of contributing editors including Conrad Aiken, Randolph Bourne, Padraic Colum and Van Wyck Brooks. In 1918, the magazine moved to New York where it became a journal of liberal opinion, its editors now including John Dewey, Thorstein Veblen, Clarence Britten, and Scofield Thayer. Among its contributors were Harold J. Laski, Charles Beard, Gilbert Seldes, and Robert Morse Lovett. By 1919, the periodical was again in financial trouble and Johnson sold it to Scofield Thayer and Dr. J. S. Watson, Jr., who were each willing to afford $25,000 annually to keep the magazine afloat.

The Johnson *Dial* had been interested in literature as it expressed American thought. The aesthetic and technical aspects of writing were ignored in favor of an examination of American thought in literature from a liberal viewpoint.

Good literature was that which expressed ideas in harmony with this viewpoint.[3]

Such criteria were not at all what Watson and Thayer had in mind. Literature as art with an emphasis upon its texture and structure, its aesthetic value as well as its content, was what interested the new editors. The first issue of their *Dial* in January, 1920, made clear that a new policy had been born. Thayer and Watson had determined to publish the best of both American and European literature, making no attempt to compromise with popular prejudice nor to support any single aesthetic school or movement. The policy earned them some furious critics. Their refusal of political propagandizing offended some people. Their publication of Europeans rankled others. Even Pound and Williams expressed vehement criticism at one time or another, although the *Dial's* credo of excellence and its openness to experiment were exactly what these men had long sought themselves. In any event, and despite critics, the *Dial* prospered.

Between 1920 and 1925, the *Dial* published just about all of those writers who have become important in modern literature: Pound, Eliot, Joyce, Stevens, Proust, Mann, Ortega, Valery, Yeats. Most of these men had been published in this country; but none, with the exception of Joyce, had gained any wide recognition until the *Dial* undertook to champion them. Eliot's "Waste Land" was published in the *Dial* in 1922, Mann's "Death in Venice" in 1924. Dos Passos, D. H. Lawrence, and Sherwood Anderson were frequent contributors. In addition, the periodical undertook to publish reproductions of modern painting, drawing and sculpture. A list of these artists includes almost every well-known name in art in the 1920s: Picasso, Chagall, de Chirico, Rousseau, Matisse, Modigliani, Marin, Burchfield, Maillol, Brancusi, Lachaise, Derain, Archipenko, to name a few.

By 1925, despite its critics, the *Dial's* prestige was formidable. Watson and Thayer's adherence to principle had resulted in a distinguished periodical that, forty-five years later, one confronts with astonishment. The combination of taste and courage in the magazine's contents is no less impressive now than it must have been in that year when the editorship passed from Thayer to Marianne Moore.

In June of 1925, Thayer announced suddenly that he would leave America to find leisure to write. Actually, he was suffering from a general breakdown, both nervous and physical, and left America to seek help from Freud in Vienna. Thayer had had an almost messianic cause in the *Dial*. He had wanted a publication flawless in every respect, one which, in presenting a synthesis of the work of the world's best minds, would effect a renaissance of the nation's spirit. The dream was enormous and its realization must, finally, have seemed impossibly difficult.

Thayer had first asked Van Wyck Brooks to replace him. William Wasserstrom says that at Thayer's request this remained a secret until, in 1958, Brooks told Gilbert Seldes who, in turn, confided the information to Wasserstrom. It seems an odd choice now, since Brooks seemed more politically oriented than Thayer. One wonders what the subsequent history of the *Dial* and, by extension, American literature might have been had Brooks accepted the job. He did not because by odd coincidence, he, too, at the time was entering a period of severe nervous breakdown. And so Marianne Moore became editor.

The July 1925 *Dial* was the first to appear with Miss Moore as editor. She shared her editorial duties with Dr. Watson, although he was, by this time, living in Rochester. Miss Moore has said, "I didn't know that Rochester was about a night's journey away, and I would say to Doctor Watson, 'Couldn't you come in for a make-up meeting, or send us these manuscripts and say what you think of them?'"

Their collaboration progressed smoothly nonetheless. Miss Moore claims that she never independently accepted a manuscript, but would submit her own feelings about it to Watson, never disguising those feelings one way or the other. She seems always to have been concerned for Watson's preferences even when they were not her own, but one has a suspicion that there were times when fast footwork was required of Watson to circumvent her objections. Witness this letter from Watson which Wasserstrom quotes: "I hope you will not feel that I am acting unconscientiously but when I reread this XXII canto it seemed . . . we really must have it for February or March and in the enthusiasm of the moment I wrote Pound much to that effect without also implying that there had been any doubt in the matter." To which Miss Moore responded, "It is I who am lacking in conscience, for disapproving of the Canto, and yet being delighted to have it."

Watson was an admirer of Pound. He was interested in the effects of Freud on the study of literature and of the possible application of scientific knowledge to criticism. Under the pseudonym of W. C. Blum, he had translated Rimbaud's *A Season in Hell* for the *Dial*. Miss Moore, on the other hand, was closer to Thayer in her interest in textual analysis. The work itself, its structure and language, concerned her more than the theories that could be discovered about it. This is not to say that her stress upon the formal elements of a work was as stringent as that of the new critics. Her critical essays, while discussing form and technique, rely heavily on her personal responses, taste, and sensitivity, but they do not stray far from the work she is discussing.

Thayer had left a detailed list of "General Instructions" for his successor. He maintained that each issue of the *Dial* should itself be a work of art, no less well made than the best work it published. Thus, the instructions dealt at length and in detail with the actual format of the journal. Verse was to be used like illustrations to break up long prose pieces. Long pieces of fiction should not be juxtaposed. Sculpture should be placed against a black or white background; bronze against white; marble against black. There was to be an alternation of impressionistic and realistic figures and of figures and landscape. Every fact and quotation was to be checked for accuracy. From 1925 until the magazine's final issue in 1929, Miss Moore scrupulously followed Thayer's "General Instructions."

Thayer's taste in the plastic arts continued to rule at the *Dial* as did his strictures about the magazine's make-up. The *Dial's* art critic, Henry McBride, continued to write commentary for the new editors, but some of his favorites, Miro, for example, were not chosen for reproduction. Thayer's preferences in this area were held sacred.

Miss Moore has described the atmosphere of the *Dial* office as it was in those years:

I think of the compacted pleasantness of those days at 152 West Thirteenth Street; of the three-story brick building with carpeted stairs, fireplace and white-mantlepiece rooms, business office in the first story front parlor, and in gold-leaf block letters, THE DIAL, on the windows to the right of the brownstone steps leading to the front door. There was the flower-crier in summer, with his slowly moving wagon of pansies, petunias, ageratum; of a man with straw-*ber*-ies for sale; or a certain fishman with pushcart-scales and staccato refrain so unvaryingly imperative, summer or winter, that Kenneth Burke's parenthetic remark comes back to me—"I think if he stopped to sell a fish my heart would skip a beat." . . . There was for us of the staff . . . a constant atmosphere of excited triumph, and from editor or publisher, inherent fireworks of parenthetic wit too good to print.[4]

Besides Miss Moore and Watson, the staff of the *Dial* in that second half of the decade was a distinguished collection. The group included Kenneth Burke, first as editorial assistant and then as music critic, replacing Paul Rosenfeld, in 1927. Henry McBride, as has been mentioned, was the *Dial's* modern art critic and Gilbert Seldes, its theater critic. These "contributing editor-critics" enjoyed, Miss Moore says, "inviolateness." "Even recklessly against the false good, they surely did represent the *Dial* in 'encouraging a tolerance of fresh experiments and opening the way for a fresh understanding of them.' "

The editors were assisted at various times in their editorial duties by Stewart Mitchell, Alyse Gregory, and Ellen Thayer (Scofield's cousin) and by Seldes and Burke as well. The list of the *Dial's* foreign correspondents during these years is remarkable: Thomas Mann for Germany, Ortega y Gasset for Madrid, John Eglinton from Dublin, Maxim Gorki from Russia, to mention a few. Eliot and Pound had commented from London and Paris respectively, but were, in these later years of the *Dial*, replaced by Raymond Mortimer and Paul Morand.

These fixed members of the staff together with the *Dial's* less frequent contributors set the tone of the magazine. Kenneth Burke, in particular, may be seen as representative. His theory of art was, in a way, a paradigm of the *Dial's* philosophy. His article, "Psychology and Form," which appeared in the July 1925 issue, had been an effort to reconcile in one aesthetic theory the seemingly conflicting interests represented, roughly, by the followers of Eliot and those of Williams. As Burke put it, he sought to reconcile "the quarrel between the aesthetes and the geneticists."

The *Dial* had always been primarily a critical review and critical essays absorbed about three-quarters of the journal's contents. The remaining portion was given over to fiction, poetry, and art reproduction. Under Miss Moore's editorship, the *Dial's* influence in criticism was expanded to include most of the important critical points of view in the twenties. She published I. A. Richards, Yvor Winters, Valéry, Aiken, Eliot, and William Carlos Williams, imposing no restraint upon their various views. Together, in a sort of grand dialogue that stretched through the many *Dial* issues between 1925 and 1929, these men sought to deal with the problems of modern literary theory. The problems themselves were described by Malcolm Cowley in the *Dial* of August 1927. The critic must, he thought, define "the relation between poetry and science, the nature of pure poetry . . . the proper function of psychology in criticism."

There were Eliot, Valéry, and Winters, on the one hand, arriving by disparate routes at a metaphysical theory of literature. Valéry, in his essay on Leonardo, argued that a close study of literature led to discovery of the Divine underlying it. Eliot, his alliance with French metaphysics intensified by his own religious conversion, saw, too, a Divine inspiration as the basis of literary excellence. Winters, though without religious connection, admitted that if one is to call one work of literature better than another, one arrives ultimately at a theistic position.

On the other hand, there were I. A. Richards and his followers, who argued for a theory of criticism grounded on no
spiritual base. They approached literature with something
like a scientific method, making a materialistic theory of
value the basis of their criticism. And then there were Williams and the men who aligned themselves with his view,
who dismissed abstractions and encompassing theories and
insisted upon consideration of the particular work.

Miss Moore gave them all room in the *Dial*. Partly, of
course, she was abiding by the spirit of the *Dial* as first envisioned by Thayer, continuing his policy of sponsoring all
points of view. But just as surely she was expressing her own
openness to intellectual experiment. She was, in her years
as editor, amazingly comprehensive in the variety of opinion
she encouraged in criticism and the formal experimentation
that she admitted in works of fiction and poetry. In only a
few areas, as we shall see, was she inflexible. In these instances it was not intellectual disagreement that was at issue,
but matters of taste in which Miss Moore's personal sensibility was offended. One can fault her for this, but the criticism
falls into insignificance beside the enormous flexibility she
displayed in most areas. Her belief, as she has stated it, was
that "if a magazine isn't to be simply a waste of good white
paper, it ought to print with some regularity, either such
work as would otherwise have to wait years for publication,
or such as would not be acceptable elsewhere."[5] And this
is what she did.

Kenneth Burke has written of Miss Moore's editorship in
his *Grammar of Motives*. When she was editor, he says,
"her ideal number . . . would I think have been one in which
all good books got long favorable reviews, all middling books
got short favorable reviews, and all books deserving of attack
were allowed to go without mention." Burke is probably accurate. There were, however, a number of writers who took
nothing like so charitable a view of Miss Moore's editorial
activities. She made some of them furious.

Miss Moore was adamant about technical precision. As
Wasserstrom says, ". . . Miss Moore was determined to dis-

cipline those writers whose loose words betrayed slovenly morals and slack minds." She had no compunctions about dissecting a piece, finding what she thought ailed it, and suggesting changes. There were contributors who were grateful or at least amenable, and there were others who got angry.

Hart Crane was one who was irate. Wasserstrom quotes his letter to Allan Tate, "How much longer [will] our market . . . be in the grip of two such hysterical virgins as the *Dial* and *Poetry!*" He had had a rather celebrated run-in with Miss Moore over his poem "The Wine Menagerie." It is difficult to know exactly what happened in this case. Crane submitted the poem and Miss Moore suggested changes including, apparently, a new title. Crane expressed gratitude to her, but fury to others.

Philip Horton, in his biography *Hart Crane*, speaks of Miss Moore's notorious editorial presumption. He says she insisted upon changes that included excision of about half the original poem as well as a new title. Crane, Horton says, was in desperate need of money and was, thus, forced to accept Miss Moore's terms.

Crane expressed his anger to others, but he did write Miss Moore, after the changes were completed, expressing his admiration for her rearrangement and agreeing that the revised poem, now titled "Again," preserved the essential spirit of the original. (However, when he reprinted the poem in book form, he used the earlier version.)

Miss Moore, speaking of the same incident, said:

Hart Crane complains of me? Well, I complain of *him*. He liked the *Dial* and we liked him—friends, and with certain tastes in common. He was in dire need of money. It seemed careless not to so much as ask if he might like to make some changes ("like" in quotations). His gratitude was ardent and later his repudiation of it commensurate—he perhaps being in both instances under a disability with which I was not familiar . . . Really I am not used to having people in that bemused state. He was so *anxious* to have us take that thing, and so *delighted*. "Well, if you would modify it a little," I said, "we would like it better."

Later Crane submitted "At Melville's Tomb" to the *Dial*

and Miss Moore replied that she would accept it, omitting the fourth stanza (an inexplicable proviso, to my mind). By now, however, she was wary and added that he was free to submit the poem elsewhere if he felt he could not comply. The poem was published in *Poetry* with an appended exegesis, by the author, that *Poetry's* editor, Harriet Monroe, had required.

In the end Miss Moore printed several of Crane's best things: "To Brooklyn Bridge," "Repose of Rivers," and "Powhatan's Daughter." Miss Moore has said of Crane, "I took a great liking to Hart Crane. . . . And Doctor Watson and Scofield Thayer liked him—felt that he was one of our talents, that he couldn't fit himself into an IBM position to find a livelihood; that we ought to, whenever we could, take anything he sent us." And of the poem, "To Brooklyn Bridge": ". . . *The Bridge* is a grand theme. Here and there I think he could have firmed it up. A writer is unfair to himself when he is unable to be hard on himself."

Miss Moore minimizes the extent of her editorial interjections. Asked whether she sought revisions from many poets, she said, "No. We had an inflexible rule: do not ask changes of so much as a comma. Accept it or reject it." And yet we know of numbers of instances when she did, in fact, ask for extensive revision.

There is a letter from Archibald MacLeish thanking Miss Moore for liking his poem "Nocturne" and authorizing her to drop the four lines she mentioned and to change the title. She suggested to Thomas Mann that the name of his character, Lorlykins, in "Disorder and Early Sorrow" be changed to "Lorlette." Mann's translator, H. G. Scheffaurer, apparently was offended by the suggestion and, according to Miss Moore, "excoriated" her. Mann offered the substitute, "Lorli," which another editor accepted in Miss Moore's absence. In the final proofs the name turned up as "Lorlikins," which Miss Moore agreed was suitable in the new spelling. What happened in this case is uncertain, but Miss Moore has spoken of Schaufaurer's "joyous subsequent retraction of abuse, and his pleasure in the narrative."

She, herself, remembers having asked for certain revisions from Gilbert Seldes and from Mark Van Doren. In 1926, she returned a number of poems to Yeats because she felt that there were some she could not publish and she did not wish to choose others from the lot.

Hemingway always felt that the *Dial* neglected his work. He submitted one or two war sketches which were rejected, but between 1924 and 1929 the *Dial* reviewed nearly all he wrote. As early as 1924, Edmund Wilson had devoted an essay in the *Dial* to Hemingway's work. Nevertheless, in the 1930s, late in the evening at a party given by the *Dial's* ex-music critic, Paul Rosenfeld, Hemingway called Miss Moore to complain. He offered to send a taxi for her if she would come tell him why the *Dial* had not published his work. He had some idea that the rejections were at her suggestion, which, in fact, they may well have been. The only record we have of Miss Moore's expressing an opinion about whether or not to accept a Hemingway piece is in a note in answer to Watson and Thayer. She wrote that she had read the piece with interest but that, as it stood, she would reject it.[6]

D. H. Lawrence, writing to Miss Moore in 1929 about poems of his she had chosen and ones that she had not, said, "I knew some of the poems would offend you. But then some part of life must offend you too. . . . Nothing is without offense, & nothing should be: if it is part of life, & not merely abstraction."[7]

Some of Miss Moore's accepting and rejecting seems to have been governed by an overscrupulosity in matters of sex. One suspects that this was true in the case of the Yeats poems that she found herself unable to print and, perhaps, had something to do with the absence of Hemingway's work. While greatly admiring Pound's Cantos, she felt constrained to say of them, "Unprudency is overemphasized and secularity persists" and, referring to Cantos XIV and XV, "Let us hope that 'Disgust with the sordid is but another expression of a sensitiveness to the finer thing,'" and "Stock oaths, and the result is ennui, as with the stock adjective."[8] This last objection may be based entirely upon a linguistic argument, although it is hard to think of an instance in Pound's Cantos where an esoteric oath might be substituted for the common one with as good effect.

Miss Moore knew what she wanted. According to Watson she had a "genius' disdain for the sanctity of genius."[9] She did not doubt the standards by which she judged contributors, feeling that she was maintaining standards handed on to her by Thayer and Watson. She must, she admits, have seemed quarrelsome to some contributors. She approached their work with a jeweler's eye for imprecision, wanting not to rewrite the piece in her own way, but to intensify the effect of what was there. She had then as she has now "nothing more than solicitude that all of us may write better." But write better than what? As editor, Miss Moore says she was "desirous of maintaining the standard and style of writing which Doctor Watson and Mr. Thayer regard as essential." But she was clearly more than a handmaiden of Thayer and Watson. She was, as they were, committed to a theory of excellence that all three felt was both demonstrable and inviolate. The implication here is that some sort of absolute standard exists by which literature may be judged.

In the 1960s such a position was unfashionable, but in the 1920s it was common. Literature was, in many ways, a citadel to be protected from the barbarians. There were rules and there were standards and many of the people involved in literary reviews saw themselves as defenders of the faith. What is amazing about the *Dial* compared to other reviews is that, even though it was imbued with this attitude, it managed to find virtue in such a diversity of work. Its standard of excellence was broad enough to encompass a great variety and, thus, Wasserstrom can say of it, "no rival journal at its best outmatched the *Dial* at its worst."

Had the standards of the *Dial* been somewhat more flexible the journal might not in its last years have become, to quote Eliot's *Criterion*, "tired." Wasserstrom believes that during Miss Moore's tenure the *Dial* lost zeal. It acquired "a taste for discrimination, for technical systems which would expand and refine the arts of criticism . . ." but it chose a middle-of-

the-road position that came down more often on the side of
the tried and safe than of the daring.

One choice in particular is noteworthy in the last years of
the *Dial*. In July 1926, Sylvia Beach wrote to Miss Moore
offering her 30–34,000 words of a new book by Joyce. Miss
Beach offered the piece to the *Dial* because she felt it was
the best of the literary reviews and, so, the most appropriate
place for the work to be published. The piece was the Shaun
chapters from "Anna Livia Plurabelle," from the work eventually published as *Finnegans Wake.*

Miss Moore wired that she was interested but would have
to see the manuscript. The manuscript was sent. In August,
Miss Moore wrote Miss Beach, accepting the manuscript
for publication. Apparently Miss Moore had read the manuscript originally during a visit in Maine without fully understanding the contents. Upon rereading the chapters she became
concerned about their suitability for the *Dial*. She feared
Thayer's reaction to their publication and with some reason.
Although Thayer had been an outspoken defender of *Ulysses,*
he had admitted that probably he would not have printed
the Nausicaa portion in the *Dial*.

Miss Moore expressed her fear to Watson, who wired that
Thayer would probably not be concerned either way. Watson
suggested printing the manuscript, using asterisks for particular
words or phrases. Miss Moore was unconvinced. She told
Sylvia Beach that the *Dial* would have to omit a third to a
half of the manuscript if it was to publish it. She inquired
whether Joyce would want to withdraw the manuscript or
would want to see it with the required omissions subject to
withdrawal. Joyce wished to withdraw the piece.

Miss Moore once again wrote Watson, disturbed to have to
reject a work that Watson evidently very much wanted to
publish, disturbed because she herself could admire Joyce's
technique if not his matter. In addition, she felt disgraced to
have to retract her acceptance of the work, but retract it
she did.

Loyalty to Thayer coincided with Miss Moore's own scruples
in this instance. Wasserstrom cites the incident as decisive to

the *Dial*, "for want of a Joyce, the *Dial* was lost." The rejection, at any rate, indicated the direction the *Dial* would take in its last years. Miss Moore willingly granted technical freedom but she was unable to approve a like freedom of content.

The last years of the *Dial* mirrored the conservative yet lively mind that guided it. Wasserstrom says,

In that final year, 1928–29, it attracted and printed materials less portentous than Eliot chose for *The Criterion*, less contentious than . . . *The Symposium*, and less prescient than R. P. Blackmur would place in *Hound and Horn*. But no other journal managed to be both wide and deep, austere and ornamental.

The magazine published Pound's translations of Cavalcante with commentary, Mann's essay on Tolstoy, Paul Claudel's essay on Japanese art, together with three pieces by Noguchi. Writers such as Jean Toomer, Albert Halper, Stanley Kunitz, and Louis Zukofsky were included side by side with Aiken, Eliot, Lawrence, Crane, Williams, and Winters. Joe Gould, the Greenwich Village philosopher, was given space. Artists such as Picasso, Modigliani, Maillol, and Bonnard continued to be represented. At the end of each issue Miss Moore included an essay of her own about some event, place, person, idea or word that had taken her fancy: Dürer's prints, an exhibit at the New York Public Library, or the abuse of circus animals. This is scarcely dull fare, but by 1929 it had become respectable. The *Dial* offerings occupied, indeed, a safe middle-of-the-road position.

The July 1929 issue was the *Dial's* last. It has been suggested that money was the problem and that the crash the following autumn was somehow responsible for the *Dial's* demise. Apparently the country's economic troubles had nothing to do with the decision to stop publishing. Watson felt that the magazine had accomplished its purpose. It is possible that the cautious approach being followed editorially led him to believe that other newer magazines could better serve the cause of experimentation.

Watson worried, too, about the burdensomeness of Miss

Moore's duties as editor. She had published no poetry during her years with the *Dial* and Watson evidently thought that this was an unfortunate situation for so good a poet. Miss Moore, on the other hand, would have liked to continue. She was enjoying the work, as her nostalgic essay, *"The Dial: A Retrospect,"* indicates.

Nevertheless, Watson determined to stop publication. He conferred with Thayer's mother to whom he proposed the idea of publishing the *Dial* as a quarterly as an alternative to discontinuing it. Thayer's mother could not agree to the alteration and in July 1929, the doors of the *Dial* were closed.

Although Miss Moore had published no poetry during these years, she had, in a very real sense, made the *Dial* her creation. Her personality was everywhere in the magazine: in the choice of contributors, in the standard of technical excellence that she required, in the arbitrarily chosen and often eccentrically juxtaposed works the journal offered. George Saintsbury and Ezra Pound appeared together, Joe Gould and Eliot. Her own taste for irregularity, variety, diversity became the guiding principle of the *Dial.* Genius was embraced where it occurred. If this meant odd bedfellows, that was of no concern to Miss Moore. She wanted precision and order. She wanted ardor and intensity. She wanted material to be of general interest, not narrowed to the concerns of a few people or a small literary movement. She wanted, in short, the best that was being written. And because her mind is both broad and profound, she found that excellence in a great variety of work. She wrote once, in reply to the *New Republic's* criticism that the *Dial* had encouraged no new writers since 1920, that the *Dial* was "a selection not of writers but of writing." [10] Work which met her standards, she took. Work that fell short, she ignored, regardless of the writer's reputation or lack of it.

Her poetry shows these same characteristics. It is constructed of diverse facts and varied observations. The whole is connected not by theory but by an underlying sense of essential similarity. The underlying similarity that joins the variety of work published in the *Dial* is excellence. One has a sense of the work's having been chosen and published in an effort to display the best being produced. There is work that one might have hoped to see in the *Dial*, work rejected, one feels, through bad judgment. Some work appears that might better, perhaps, have been rejected, whose quality is not on a par with other things. But overall the quality is staggering. The 1925–29 issues stand as a monument to one woman's judgment. As Wasserstrom points out, these issues comprise a sort of poem—Marianne Moore's poem called the *Dial*.

CHAPTER VI ✌ SELECTED POEMS
1935

✌ *MARIANNE MOORE'S* professional editing ended with the close of the *Dial*, although in 1931 and 1932 Pound suggested her as a possible successor to Harriet Monroe at *Poetry*. She returned to writing poetry, occasional essays and book reviews, work that has occupied her without interruption to the present time.

In 1929, Miss Moore and her mother moved from the Greenwich Village apartment they had occupied since 1918 to a fifth-floor apartment in Brooklyn on Cumberland Street where Miss Moore continued to live for most of the next forty years. Her brother, John, was stationed by that time at the Brooklyn Navy Yard. Her mother was not well. These facts may have contributed to the decision to move to Brooklyn, but, in a sense, the move had a symbolic fitness. The Village years were over, figuratively as well as literally. The concerns of the next decade were distant from the concerns of the twenties.

Cumberland Street is, today, a tough section. Violence in all its big-city forms is not uncommon. But, Miss Moore says, in 1929:

decorum marked the life on Clinton Hill. . . . An atmosphere of privacy with a touch of diffidence prevailed, as when a neighbor in furred jacket, veil, and gloves would emerge from a four-story house to shop at grocer's or meat-market . . . It was not unusual in those days, toward teatime, to catch a glimpse of a maid with starched cap and apron, adjusting accessories on a silver tray . . .[1]

When I visited her there in 1960, the yellow stone of Miss Moore's narrow apartment was grayed by soot. Two globes that she has called "mothballs"[2] flanked the entrance on iron stands. The globes have been broken often in recent times. The building's lobby has been set afire by vandals. Five floors above, the apartment seemed aloof from such violence. It was furnished, as one would expect it to be, with a random mixture of things, somehow all seeming to have grown there. There were dozens of small animals in glass, ivory and ebony and there were pictures of animals—kangaroos and porcupines. There was heavy dark furniture as well as a sofa and chair of fruitwood, French, Miss Moore thinks, given to her mother by a friend. There was a variety of paintings—the heavy tea-colored oils that Americans hung before the First World War, and a painting that Mabel Dodge sent her from Mexico. There were, of course, books, stacks of them everywhere. "We mix our furniture systematically because we can not help it,"[3] Miss Moore once said.

"We," of course, meant Miss Moore and her mother, for whom she had great affection and respect. Mrs. Moore read all of her daughter's poems while they were being written and offered criticism that was frequently heeded. Miss Moore tells of a line she once wrote, " 'the adder and the child with a bowl of porridge' " to which her mother responded with, " 'It won't do.' " That was the end of that line.[4]

Her mother seems to have had some of Miss Moore's own dislike for the imprecise word. She spoke of being tired of the word *sincere*.[5] Miss Moore thought this was a word she could not do without, but worked at it until she had analyzed it into other meanings.

Miss Moore's brother, John, was another critic whose judgment she respected. When worried about a poem, she often sought his advice, as in the case of "The Buffalo," which she thought might sound too jerky. Her brother replied that it quite took his fancy and this set her at ease.

A reverence for language was, one suspects, something of a family preoccupation. Marguerite Young, in a reminiscence that she wrote for Miss Moore's seventy-seventh birthday, recalls how Miss Moore and her mother had spoken together in a language that might have been plucked from a poem. The commonest daily business was transacted in sentences that were flights of imagination. She recalls a time when they both had had long colds and were afraid to go about for fear of infecting other people, until one day when Mrs. Moore said, "Let us have done with the umbrella of our contagion."[6]

The move to Brooklyn was congenial to both of them. They enjoyed the anonymity and the lessening of pressure that Brooklyn provided after New York. It was a place, Miss Moore has said, that afforded the kind of tame excitement on which she thrives.

In the comparative peace of Brooklyn, Miss Moore began writing poems again after the hiatus of the *Dial* years. By 1934 friends were urging her to put together another book, the last book having been published a decade earlier. As in the case of both *Poems* and *Observations*, there were friends ready to take on the job themselves, including, this time, Robert Frost. But in 1934 arrangements had already been made to bring out a *Selected Poems* which was to be published by Macmillan in America and by Faber and Faber in England. The book appeared in 1935. It contained most of the poems from *Poems* and *Observations* and added nine new ones. T. S. Eliot, as I have noted, wrote the Introduction to the English *Selected Poems* which contains the much-quoted statement: "Miss Moore's poems form part of the small body of durable poetry written in our time."

To the new book Miss Moore appended a postscript, offered instead of a dedication. "Dedications," it says, "imply giving, and we do not care to make a gift of what is insufficient; but in my immediate family there is one 'who thinks in a particular way'; and I should like to add that where there is an effect of thought or pith in these pages, the thinking and often the actual phrases are hers." That person was, of course, her mother.

Of the nine new poems in the *Selected Poems*, several are, I think, among the best fifteen or twenty Miss Moore has written. If there is one general criticism to be made about the early poems, it is that some of them were almost too spare: although Miss Moore has named compression as the first grace of style, too much compression can be arid. Abstraction, concision, and dry wit are carried to extremes in some of these early poems ("To a Steam Roller," "Nothing Will Cure the Sick Lion," "The Past is the Present," "Injudicious Gardening," for example). It is as though in these small acid poems Miss Moore is trying to be "modern" more than she is trying to be herself. In the newer poems there is an opening out from this rather too constrained style. The lyric warmth that appeared like tropical oases in such poems as "People's Surroundings" and "Marriage" occurs more often. A kind of affectionate humor begins to supplant sharp wit. There is a feeling of ampleness and leisure in the comparatively longer lines of these comparatively longer poems.

Actually the lines may not be much longer and one can find several long poems among the earlier ones, but the new poems *feel* more leisurely. If changes of this kind were noticed in a woman's face, one might say the face had softened, but the word would be misleading used in reference to the poetry. The same clear-edged language appears in the same intricately —perhaps more intricately—constructed line. It is the effect that is different. The poems seem to come from a gentler hand, one more self-assured.

Some of the first members of Miss Moore's famous bestiary appear in the new poems. Of the nine poems, four have as heroes exotic creatures: a jerboa, a plumet basilisk, a frigate pelican, and an Indian buffalo. One can scarcely think of more unlikely subjects for poetry, but that, perhaps, is the point. These creatures, by virtue of their rarity, exist unencumbered by the preconceptions people have about commoner animals. Unlike a cat or a dog or a cow, a jerboa is an unknown quantity; hardly anyone has preconceptions about what qualities are jerboa-like. A rare animal, like a word stripped to its exact meaning, can be used to say precisely what the poet

wants to say. There will not be danger of the meaning's being muddled by a baggage of previous associations that a
commoner animal would be bound to bring along.

The creatures in Miss Moore's animal kingdom have qualities that she would find agreeable in human beings. It is a
kingdom where only brave, restrained, and self-sufficient animals are admitted. They go about their business with an
efficiency that Miss Moore finds admirable. In later poems the
animals are often armored with scales or quills or some other
means of self-protection. They are equipped to take care of
themselves in a world that seems increasingly dangerous.

Danger, unspecific but pervasive, is another theme that
turns up in these new poems. In such earlier poems as "The
Fish" and "A Grave," the danger was specifically the sea.
In "The Steeple Jack" danger is the subject but its source is
vague. It is a threat that is everywhere just under the surface
tranquillity of the town and which the town's tidy fresh-paint
formality just barely controls. "The Hero," too, is a poem
woven around the nebulous dreads of nightmare. The dangers
here are, in part, like childhood spooks, things that go bump
in the night. The hero is he who can, by force of will, master
the danger. Like the armored animals that appear later, the
hero withstands the amorphous dangers of life by hardening
himself against them.

"The Steeple Jack" and "The Hero" are two portions of a
three-part piece published originally in 1932 and called "Part
of a Novel, Part of a Poem, Part of a Play." The third part,
"The Student," was not reprinted until it appeared in 1941 in
What Are Years. Miss Moore has said that the title given the
three-part poem is "all too truthful." She confesses to having
wanted to write fiction and if not fiction, plays, and says that
verse struck her as next best. These poems *are* like scenes
from a play or a novel, stage sets in which the central action
is implicit, about to begin.

Two things strike one immediately, I think, in "The Steeple-
Jack": first, the visual quality of the poem. In the first line
the scene is suggested as a view that would please the painter,
Dürer, and throughout the rest of the poem Miss Moore's

.

own painter's eye is at work. We are offered an American
primitive canvas in which the sea is etched with waves "as
formal as the scales / on a fish." It is "a sea the purple of
the peacock's neck" and is "paled to greenish azure as Dürer
changed / the pine green of the Tyrol to peacock blue and
guinea / grey." There is a list of old-fashioned flowers. There
is a summer house shaped like "an antique / sugar-bowl."
"Boats / at sea progress white and rigid as if in / a groove."
The steeplejack, himself, is dressed in scarlet, gilding a star
on the church steeple, posting a danger sign that is white and
red. One can *see* this place, its church and its lighthouse and
its "moon-vines trained on fishing twine."

Next, one sees that the scene might have come straight out
of Hans Christian Andersen. It is a storybook town in all its
painted primary-color exactness. The eight stranded whales
one may see there is a fairytale touch, combining the fan-
tastic with the prosaic as children's stories do. The steeplejack
called C. J. Poole, the student called Ambrose, the fact that
whales were exactly eight all have the gratuitously specific
quality of nursery tales.

The last stanza of the poem begins with the startling lines:
"It could not be dangerous to be living / in a town like this."
Well, of course not, whoever thought it was? But Miss Moore
must have thought so to have written the lines, which are
worded as though spoken by a child with crossed fingers.

To a child, or to the child who lives within us all, the
world has evident danger that does not need to be articulated. As adults we call it death or bankruptcy and say that
our fears are logical, but these fears come from the same
irrational source as the unspecific hobgoblins of childhood.
An amorphous danger, implicit in the very act of living, is
the sort of thing Miss Moore seems half to expect even in
such tranquillity.

There are a number of ways of armoring against fear. One
of the best is to construct a world for oneself that seems to
operate logically. The town of "The Steeple-Jack" is such a
world, orderly and formal and controlled, where even the
waves of the ocean have been tamed to imitate the formal

scales of fish, where even the vegetation and the animals
are docile, unlike their unrestrained tropical counterparts.
The only disruption is an occasional storm that bends the
marsh grass and disturbs the steeple's star. It is a "whirlwind
fife-and-drum," this storm—a Fourth of July parade-like storm,
loud and boisterous, then, but not serious. Of it Miss Moore
says, "it is a privilege to see so / much confusion." In a
town like this a summer storm constitutes "so much confusion." *But,* Miss Moore seems to be saying, this is really
a storybook town, a pleasant fiction, a charming picture painted
not from reality but from wishful thinking.

The steeplejack, who gilds the star that stands for hope,
posts a danger sign below his work. Where is the danger? It
must be in the very burnishing of hope, another activity that
wards off fear but is perhaps also a kind of fiction, "hope
not being hope / until all ground for hope has / vanished—"
as the poem "The Hero" says.

"It could not be dangerous to be living / in a town like
this" thus becomes an ironic statement, doubling the meaning
back on itself. The means taken to protect against danger
become, themselves, the final danger. They are fictions and
cannot be trusted to protect.

The "Steeple-Jack" that appears in the *Selected Poems* is a
shortened version of the original. The cut lines were re-
stored when the poem was printed again in 1961 in *A Marianne Moore Reader* and this is the version that appears in
the *Complete Poems.* I am glad Miss Moore chose to restore
the lines or we would have missed the wonderful catalog of
vegetation in the sixth stanza which, while perhaps non-
essential, is so pretty in its wild variety.

The hero of the second poem is the man who is able to
live without fictions. He takes life as it is, seeing "the rock /
crystal thing to see."

The first two stanzas of this poem detail frightening things.
One should say "scary" things, because the list is a child's
list: "weeds of beanstalk height," the wind that has a " 'scare-
babe voice,' " an owl's eyes in a yew tree, "deviating head-
stones," "standing and listening where something / is hiding."

The hero, himself, "shrinks / as what it is flies out on muffled wings." As a child is scared by what he cannot quite see, so an adult is frightened by mystery. But, just as in "The Steeple-Jack" a facade of order was a storybook fiction, so a world without mystery is a fiction.

Being alive entails being afraid, disliking some of the things one has to do. The hero is the person who can see life whole, realizing that the mysterious inner world produces the brimming light of an El Greco as well as the thing that flies out on muffled wings. Where there is fear, "love won't grow." Accepting life whole is the condition of being a hero. One must be afraid and stand it, do one's duty in spite of dislike, be tolerant of one's fellow creatures, and, like the frock-coated Negro serving as guide at Washington's grave, have a "sense of human dignity / and reverence for mystery."

Both "The Steeple-Jack" and "The Hero" are written in syllabic lines with the occasional eccentric line-breaks that the syllable count requires. There is an odd sort of cadence to poetry written in syllabics. The reader knows that some control of rhythm is being used, but the effect is much subtler than in a usual metric line. If these poems are read with a slight pause at the line end, the effect is eccentric indeed, odd words take on emphasis and one has a sense of being jerked along. Sometimes this jerky progression is pleasant, sometimes funny and, occasionally, irritating. Syllabic verse is intended primarily for the eye: the pattern it makes on a page is part of its charm. It is a verse form not nearly as congenial to the mouth and ear. Miss Moore is in general a poet of the eye. She tells you how things look, not how they sound or feel or taste. She paints pictures as detailed as old botanical prints, as brightly colored as Persian miniatures. She is a poet of the eye, but not *entirely* of the eye. There are poems in which the rhythm is so elegant, the sound of the words so delicate that they take your breath. "The Jerboa" is one of these.

Eliot said of "The Jerboa" that it would be difficult to define its subject. It has to do with naturalness and artifice, with the decadent luxury of the Pharaohs and the Spartan but ample life of the little desert animal. Miss Moore, of course, prefers the simple, natural thing. This, then, is what the poem is "about," but really the poem is about the wonders that can be worked with words and rhythms.

The poem is strictly constructed, all twenty-six stanzas are of the same length, there is no variation whatsoever in the syllable count of parallel lines, the rhyme scheme remains the same. Amazing things happen within this framework. The first seventeen stanzas are slow paced, the last nine are quick and sprightly, the rhythm in each case suited to the subject. And yet, there has been not a syllable added to or subtracted from any stanza in the poem. The effect of varying tempo is done entirely by word sounds. The first seventeen stanzas contain long or longish words, one whole line, for example, made of the word "hippopotami." There are many vowels in these stanzas, long *o*'s, long *a*'s and long *i*'s as compared to the pattern of consonants, *d*'s, *t*'s, *b*'s and *s*'s in particular, in the last nine stanzas. Compare these lines of equal syllable length: "poetry of frog grays" to "neatly back and blending" or "limes, and pomegranates" to "to the flageolet." All the encumbered pomp of the Pharoahs is in the words, all the freedom of the jerboa.

There is a kind of undulating elegance in a line like "on a three-cornered smooth-working Chippendale / claw." A parallel line from another stanza says, "is buff-brown like the breast of the fawn-breasted / bower-bird" and the effect is quite different because of the kinds of words used.

There is pleasure in particular groups of words: "Lords and ladies put goose-grease / paint in round bone boxes— the pivoting / lid incised with a duck-wing" or "the pig-tailed monkey on / slab hands, with arched-up slack-slung gait." And there is pleasure in the use of single words as, for instance, "Chippendale" to describe the jerboa's claw, so incongruous but, on second thought, so exactly right. Here is nature imitating art in the last stanza, a neat touch in a poem that has devoted seventeen stanzas to detailing the perversions art has made of nature.

Visual detail is not missing. The jerboa makes "fern-seed

/ footprints." There are "frog grays, / duck-egg greens, and eggplant blues." Wild ostriches rear back their necks "like a serpent preparing to strike." The jerboa itself is described with all the detailed precision of a natural history book.

A preference for the natural rather than the overrefined is the theme of the following poem as well. The "Camellia Sabina" of the title is a pampered, overrefined flower which Miss Moore likens to grapes used for wine, both having been perverted from their natural state by human artifice. Miss Moore describes the care of the flower, using information taken from the Abbé Barlèse's monograph on camellias. The care of the grape is described in words from *The Epicure's Guide to France.* Characteristically, there are also the bits of information from the *National Geographic* and several other sources.

I would prefer not to go too deeply into the poem's argument for the superiority of the "food grape." Miss Moore is no wine-lover and her argument rests on this preference. She finds nothing wrong with pampering a grape that is intended for eating, although similar pampering of a wine-destined grape annoys her. Nevertheless, the poem can be read with perfect pleasure even while one finds its logic a little cockeyed. It is funny in its deliberate eccentricity. Miss Moore says that "the French are a cruel race": they are "willing / to squeeze the diner's cucumber . . ." And of wine she says it accomplishes nothing but making the soul heavy, "though the / history *de la Vigne et du vin* has placed a *mirabelle* in the *bibliothèque.*"

The lines are quite long, suitable to a meditative poem. The version that appears in the *Complete Poems* has been made even more leisurely by the stanzaic rearrangement of the original eight lines so that they appear as nine. The tone is, by comparison to the three previous poems, somewhat prosy. There are, nonetheless, some lovely images: for example, "this graft-grown briar-black bloom / on blackthorn pigeon's-blood." There are the lines: "with amanita-white petals; there are several of her / pale pinwheels, and pale / stripe that looks as if on a mushroom the / sliver from a beetroot carved into a rose were laid." And there is the description of a "mouse with a / grape in its hand and its child / in its mouth" which Miss Moore thinks looks like the "Spanish fleece suspended by the neck."

The poem is not a great one, but it is charming. One aspect of it bothers me, however. I object to referring to a mouse as "the Prince of Tails" and to the whole concept of Tom Thumb riding around under the grape leaves. These things, it seems to me, constitute mere whimsy. This rarely happens in Miss Moore's poetry, but when, as here, it does, it is as jarring as finding a picture made of sea shells hanging in the Louvre. One expects, unreasonably, invariably perfect taste from Miss Moore. I suppose that is because one nearly always gets it.

"No Swan So Fine" is another unfavorable comparison of the natural and the artificial. No live swan is so fine as the "chintz china" one at Versailles, Miss Moore says ironically. The poem begins, " 'No water is so still as the / dead fountains of Versailles.' " It ends a stanza later with the comment, "The king is dead." One thinks of the lines from "To Statecraft Embalmed," "As if a death-mask ever could replace / life's faulty excellence!" For Miss Moore flawed reality is invariably preferable to the perfection of art. Better always than chintz china is the real swan "with swart blind look askance / and gondoliering legs."

When one pauses to think about these last three poems, one finds something ironic about a criticism of artifice imbedded in such superrefined stanzas. One wonders why Miss Moore is writing poetry at all if she disapproves so strongly of artifice. Is poetry any less an artifice than other kinds of art? Is all art then a kind of death mask? Perhaps Miss Moore would make an exception for art enlivened with the spirit of its creator to such an extent that it ceases to be a death mask. But even then isn't the life of the work something quite different from life itself? Perhaps, in fact, Miss Moore does not disapprove of artifice at all. These are some of the questions that the poems raise, whether intentionally or not. It is typical of Miss Moore's poetry that the meaning is equivocal. As in her essays, as, in fact, in her most casual comments, the ambiguity of her meaning dawns slowly. She gives and takes away in the same motion so that often, just as one believes he understands, the words start to fold back on themselves and an exactly opposite meaning begins to seem plausible.

For example, one could read "No Swan So Fine" straight, with no irony intended. Miss Moore plainly says that no live swan is so fine as the china one on a candelabrum. We assume irony partly because we have read others of her poems dispraising artificiality, partly because of the ambiguity of the word "fine," but mostly because of the suggestions of death in the first and last lines. Miss Moore *could* be saying— probably is not but *could* be—that art is preferable to life because, unlike natural things that die, it is everlasting (note the flowers, "everlastings," on the candelabrum). One could make a case for this interpretation. We only *assume* irony.

"The Jerboa," "Camellia Sabina," and "No Swan So Fine" are top-of-the-mind poems: the content exists largely on the surface and can be grasped purely by the intellect. These poems do not have the sense of hidden content that haunts "A Grave." "The Plumet Basilisk" is a long poem of four sections which inhabits both surface and depth and must be read with intuition as well as thought. The first and last sections of the poem, both called "In Costa Rica," have mystery. The middle sections, "The Malay Dragon" and "The Tuatera," are top-of-the-mind.

A comparison of lines from these sections is revealing. The first section begins:

In blazing driftwood
  the green keeps showing at the same place;
as, intermittently, the fire opal shows blue and green.

The second part begins:

We have ours; and they
  have theirs. Ours has a skin feather crest;
theirs has wings out from the waist which is snuff-brown or sallow.

Both passages are descriptive, but the one has the mystery of a witch's incantation. The other would not seem out of place in an encyclopedia.

The plumet basilisk is a Costa Rican lizard. The Malay dragon and the tuatera are other kinds of lizards, but they are all dragons to Miss Moore. One should remember that the title of one of Miss Moore's best-known later poems is "O To Be a Dragon," an incarnation that she would find most agreeable according to the poem, embodying both enormous power and the ability to be, at times, invisible. To be a dragon is to be secure.

> In
> Copenhagen the principal door
> of the bourse is roofed by two pairs of dragons standing on
> their heads . . . so that the four
> green tails conspiring upright, symbolize fourfold security.

As "The Plumet Basilisk" says: These lizard-dragons are amphibious, some hibernating for as long as six months under water, the Notes tell us. Miss Moore admires this quality, says "the basilisk portrays / mythology's wish / to be interchangeably man and fish." But surely it is not literally the dragon's ability to exist under water that Miss Moore envies. Water and the ability to live in it have other meanings for her.

If it is legitimate to find in recurring images recurring meaning—as I think it is—then it is legitimate to associate the water here with water as it has been used in other poems. The sea in "A Grave," in "The Fish," and in "The Steeple-Jack" come to mind. In each case the water has been threatening (or, in "The Steeple-Jack," rendered unthreatening only by the imposition of control) and has seemed, finally, to threaten out of all proportion to its real potential for harm.

For Miss Moore mystery has been the dangerous thing. There is danger in the thing not seen, as in the spooks of "The Hero." There is the felt-rather-than-seen presence of danger in "The Steeple-Jack" and "A Grave." In numbers of later poems the theme is armoring, guarding, being ready.

The means of protection are detailed. The danger is never made explicit.

To be afraid of what one cannot see or name seems ultimately, then, to be afraid of what one can imagine. When the danger is not objective, it must reside within one's own mind. In "A Grave," and in "The Fish," for instance, this sense of danger all out of proportion to reasonable expectation of harm leads me to suggest that for Miss Moore the real source of danger is contained in the mysterious promptings of her unconscious mind. Her preoccupation with formal controls would seem to imply the existence of something nearly uncontrollable. Up to this point in the poetry all emphasis has been on, first, the presence of danger and, second, on the formal means to control it. In "The Plumet Basilisk" there suddenly appears a new way of looking at the dangers of the mysterious, and there is suggested a new way of handling them. Given certain powers, one may safely embrace the danger, Miss Moore seems to say.

The water, in "The Plumet Basilisk," is calm and, although it retains mystery, it is no longer threatening. Or, rather, it is not threatening to dragons. Miss Moore's admiration for the dragon is, in part, due to his ability to immerse himself fearlessly in the mysterious element, something she seems to imply she cannot but would like to be able to do.

To be able to live thus, both on land and water, or, perhaps, on both the surface and in the depths of the mind, is heroic, almost godlike. "He leaps and meets his / likeness in the stream . . . king with king," and, "then with a spring / dives to the stream bed, hiding as the chieftain with gold body hid in / Guatavita Lake." The chieftain, here, the notes report, is a part of the legend of El Dorado. He was yearly gilded to symbolize the sun, the supreme deity. This lizard-dragon, like the chieftain or sun (and, as we will see later, like the imagination itself), is supernatural in its ability to survive in mystery.

The sea of "A Grave" was filled with the bones of drowned men. The water of "The Plumet Basilisk" hides "the yet unfound jade ax-heads, / silver jaguars and bats, and amethysts and / polished iron, gold in a ten-ton chain, and pearls the size of pigeon eggs." The treasures to be found in the inner world are as numerous as the threats. There can be safety and refuge in the depths of this place, if only one is a dragon.

This brave little dragon, Miss Moore says, is the true jewel that the Spanish conquistadors failed to recognize. With their eyes concentrated on outer things, they missed what was truly valuable. True value resides in the power that can enter the mysterious element and emerge uninjured. For a poet the treasures of this inner place are as compelling as its threats. Miss Moore knows this when she envies the dragon.

Miss Moore has been able to talk about an inner world in early poems, but in an abstract manner that recognizes without fully embracing. The great majority of the early poems are what I have chosen to call top-of-the-mind. They are characterized by intellect, wit, and a prose quality that seems determined not to let the inner world intrude. She has talked *about* the source of imagination in analyzing poetry, but has not often let this inner world expose itself in words of its own choosing. In the few poems where deep feeling is allowed irrational expression, the atmosphere is dread. In only one early poem, "Marriage," are there lines with a mysterious lyrical quality equal to those of "The Plumet Basilisk." They are lines that defy paraphrase in every case, are more like an orchestration of feeling than an expression of meaning. They seem to celebrate the mystery of feeling in images that have floated up from the underside of the mind.

There is an astonishing series of stanzas in the last section of "The Plumet Basilisk" beginning with the conceit of the basilisk's tail as piano keys. The tempo of the poem gradually speeds up, the lines becoming shorter and the stanzas irregular. The images are for the ear—drums, bagpipes, castanets, screams, whistles, and a harp. The imagery describes the dark that frightens man but that the basilisk welcomes as a refuge. The passage begins with images that are comprehensible enough but ends in pure music:

> with trees as avenues of steel to veil
black opal emerald opal

emerald—the prompt-delayed loud-
low chromatic listened-for down-
scale

The the pace gradually slows down with the lines:

which Swinburne called in prose, the
noiseless music that hangs about
the serpent when it stirs or springs.

and returns to the stanza length of the rest of the poem in the
next stanza.

The striking thing here has been the emphasis on ear, both
in the imagery and in the music of the lines themselves. The
ear is a more "sensual" organ than the eye; and hearing is
thus more closely related to emotion than is seeing. The
opening out of Miss Moore's poetry that I have said seems
to occur in this group of new poems is demonstrated here,
I think. It has to do with using words for their feeling as
well as their meaning, being willing to let the inner world
speak in its own voice. It is really a loosening of defenses
that is reflected in the rhythm of the images as well as in the
content.

"The Plumet Basilisk" is an astonishing poem, both in its
wistful recognition of the riches of mystery and in its sporadic
loosening of control. The passage that I have just quoted
could not have been written by the rational processes that
produced "To a Steam Roller." Only the unconscious mind,
magnificently, crazily, out of control, could produce lines so
opulent. The lines come from a place and speak to a place
where the rational mind has no lease. Progressively Miss Moore
is able to let this happen in her poems until, finally, in a
very late poem, she can acknowledge the irrational imagination
as both the source of danger and its means of control.

"The Frigate Pelican" that appears in the *Complete Poems*
is slightly less than half as long as the version published in
the *Selected Poems*. I guess the cutting was a good idea although the longer version has a beautiful swoop. The lines
cut served only as elaboration of things that are said simply

and at sufficient length in the shorter poem. But I regret the passing of this one line, "The reticent lugubrious ragged immense minuet," for its own sake.

The frigate pelican is not a nice bird by human standards, but that is the point. He really is not even a pelican, but a swift or perhaps a swallow, according to the long version. Humans have misnamed him and are likely to make similar mistakes about his actions if they judge them according to human values.

When the pelican gets his dinner by badgering other birds until they surrender what they have caught, he is only being true to his nature. If he is a bully by our standards, he is simply himself by his own. He is graceful, strong, and independent, making no effort to disarm or be helpful as the swan in *Hansel and Gretel*. "A less / limber animal," the human apparently, has a lot of homely mottoes to live by. Not this bird. He never heard of them and would not care if he had.

Like "impassioned Handel" the bird "hides / in the height and in the majestic / display of his art." Handel, though impassioned, we are told, was never known to fall in love; falling in love, then, being regarded as—like homely mottoes and the unreal swan of the nursery tale—a species of human sentimentalizing not dignified by passion. The Hindu saying, " 'If I do well I am blessed / whether any bless me or not, and if I do / ill I am cursed,' " is a motto more befitting a pelican.

This poem is a good example of Miss Moore's typical ambiguity. On the one hand, she is saying birds are not people and that their behavior is improperly discussed in human terms. On the other hand, she seems to imply that the bird's qualities would not be unpleasant to find in human beings. The bird's unconfidingness is likened to Handel's. Suddenly one has the idea that human traits of certain kinds *can* be discussed in relation to the pelican. Perhaps, then, any creature who would forego sentimentalizing his behavior and act according to his nature would behave like the pelican. Who can say for sure? In this poetry nothing is simple, including the Notes to this poem, which were not cut to conform to

the cutting of the poem itself. There are two entries in the
Notes to "The Frigate Pelican" in the *Complete Poems* which
refer to lines that are no longer included. It is hard to believe
that this is not an oversight. "Omissions are not accidents"
is the "epigraph" (signed M.M.) appearing in the front of the
book. I wonder about inclusions.

The poem "The Buffalo" celebrates the Indian buffalo
among the many other varieties of ox that exist. He is strong
and mettlesome and cheerful. He serves man well but with
independent spirit and is fierce enough to fight a tiger if
called upon to do so. Besides he is nice to look at.

The poem is attractive in its rather dainty, lady-like tone
and funny when you think of the ponderous animal it describes.

> Black in blazonry means
> prudence; and niger, unpropitious. Might
> hematite—
> black, compactly incurved horns on bison
> have significance?

And "those two horns which when a tiger / coughs, are
lowered fiercely." Very tippy-toe this style is, but not to the
point of being silly, only just enough to suggest that the
buffalo's fan is a lady.

"Nine Nectarines" was called "Nine Nectarines and Other
Porcelain" in the *Selected Poems*. Its title was "Nine Nectarines"
in the *Collected Poems*, "Nine Nectarines and Other Porcelain"
in *A Marianne Moore Reader*, and back to the short title in
the *Complete Poems*. Miss Moore tends to do this with titles
in the same way that she sometimes adds or subtracts quotation marks in different versions of the same poem. Sometimes it is hard to see why. In the case of "Nine Nectarines,"
the other porcelain of the title is described in the *Selected
Poems* only. These stanzas are cut from all other versions.

The object this poem describes is an old porcelain plate
decorated with nectarines on a branch. The lines cut from
the early version described other porcelain, French and English,
decorated with scenes more stolid, less imaginative. The revision both reinforces concentration upon the plate which is
the poem's subject and makes more subtle what Miss Moore

is saying about it. The unimaginative European porcelain served as an almost too obvious comparison to the imaginative subtlety of the Chinese plate.

The point here seems to be about the same as that made in "When I Buy Pictures"—that good art is that which is infused with the imaginative spirit of its creator. It is interesting to compare the two poems' methods of making the same statement.

"When I Buy Pictures" says what it has to say in prose-like sentences that would be hard to misinterpret. Miss Moore describes what she likes, mentions some qualities in pictures she does not like and ends with three lines stating exactly the quality that all pictures she admires have in common. That quality is evidence of a mind that can see "into the life of things." Miss Moore is writing criticism.

In "Nine Nectarines" she admires the Chinese plate for the imaginative mind it implies, but her method is not direct statement. The poem concentrates on a long description of the plate's decoration. The last stanza begins with the lines, "A Chinese 'understands / the spirit of the wilderness' " and ends with, "It was a Chinese / who imagined this master-piece," obliquely making the point. Miss Moore has removed all words and lines that might make the point obvious. The revision of the title makes even the fact that the subject is a plate somewhat doubtful until halfway through the poem. The result is a poem in which the poetry dominates. The theme is there only if you want to find it—implied but unobtrusive.

The method of "Nine Nectarines" might be criticized as deliberately obscuring meaning, but only if one believes that a poem has to "mean" something. The poem is hard to paraphrase. It will not be tucked neatly into a box, for some image or phrase is always hanging out. But who cares? If one wants philosophy there are plenty of essays for us to read. What we have in "Nine Nectarines" is poetry; a joy in words and rhythm, a pleasure in description. What we have, finally, is imagination itself, not talk about imagination.

CHAPTER VII ❧ THE PANGOLIN AND WHAT ARE YEARS

❧ THE PUBLICATION of the *Selected Poems* brought Miss Moore's poetry to the attention of a public wider than the literary circle who had all along admired her work. In 1935, she was awarded the Ernest Hartsock Memorial Prize for the *Selected Poems*. In 1936, the Brendin Publishing Company of London printed another small book, *The Pangolin and Other Verse*, a tiny collection of five poems, some of which were published again in 1941 in *What Are Years*. The Brendin Publishing Company was Miss Moore's old friend Bryher; designer of the book was George Plank, who came from Carlisle.

"The Pangolin" of the book's title is a lovely poem, interesting in several ways. It begins, "Another armored animal . . .," a statement perhaps partly self-mocking in light of Miss Moore's preoccupation with defenses. Really, the number of her poems that deal directly or indirectly with protection *is* astonishing. Every poem with an animal for subject is careful to mention his means of self-defense, and danger, as we have seen, is the subject or implied subject of many other poems.

If there is a theme that runs from first to last in Marianne Moore's poems, it is the theme of self-defense. The very style of the early poems is defensive, wit and irony and extreme precision being a kind of armor to hide feeling. Never quite to commit oneself is a defense. Notice in the poems the use of ambiguity, the reliance on irony which by its nature both affirms and denies, the use of paradox. A statement that is unambiguous is frequently in quotation marks, meaning that perhaps Miss Moore agrees, perhaps she doesn't, but that the responsibility for having been so blunt is someone else's. "In This Age of Hard Trying, Nonchalance is Good." Why? Because "the staff, the bag, the feigned inconsequence / of manner, best bespeak that weapon, self-protectiveness." The frigate pelican is "unconfiding" and Miss Moore approves this. She herself is unconfiding, finding in a dozen stratagems of style "that weapon, self-protectiveness."

Her admiration for armored animals is a professional's respect for another professional. Witness the loving care with which she describes the pangolin's scaly armor plate:

scale
lapping scale with spruce-cone regularity until they
form the uninterrupted central
tail-row!

I think the exclamation point is pure envy. Look at the armor Nature has provided for this animal, unrequested! Humans must devise their own.

"Armor seems extra" for this animal. He has several other means of protection as well. He can draw in his eyes, nose and ears and close them over. He can roll into a ball that cannot be unrolled and do this without breaking his neck. He has a nest of rocks which can be "closed with earth from inside." But in addition to all these riches he has scales. He looks like an artichoke. One suspects that next to being a dragon who can become invisible, Miss Moore would like best to be a pangolin. Maybe that is how she sees herself already and "another armored animal" is a cry of recognition.

Man, not nearly so well-provided with protection, has many more things to protect. Physical armor is not enough to shield a creature of intellect and emotion. Man stumbles along, sometimes funny, sometimes contemptible, lacking the grace of the pangolin.

Grace, that many-meaning word, is discussed briefly. It is the natural movement of the pangolin, a "frictionless creep . . . made graceful by adversities, con- / versities." Man finds grace in art, in character, in the forgiveness of sins and the leniency of creditors. Man's concept of grace must include spiritual grace because, unlike the pangolin, he has been given the means to appreciate it.

The gifts of brain and emotion which cause man's vulnerability to danger are, themselves, his best protection as well. He has humor, and humor "saves a few steps." He has vigor and the power to grow and can, when thwarted or defeated, look forward with hope to a new day, a new beginning.

Like the Hero of the earlier poem, Miss Moore looks "upon a fellow creature's error with the / feelings of a mother—a / woman or a cat." Her tone has changed considerably from the acidulous criticism of man's follies in *Observations*. The follies, the self-deceiving and bungling, remain unchanged, but compassion has replaced impatience in Miss Moore's view of these things. Grace is granted the graceless.

The poems in *Observations* tended to look outward and to be concerned with comment on the observable world of people and things. The style of the poetry mirrored the content in its reliance on prose-like statement and visual detail. The contemporary world of 1915–20 provided the subjects for a great many of the poems. The technical concerns of the time influenced the style.

The new poems after 1929, those nine that appear in the *Selected Poems,* represent a turning inward. They coincide with Miss Moore's own partial withdrawal from the New York literary world—her move to Brooklyn—and were written during the Depression. The subjects of the poems are no longer drawn from the contemporary world, but are timeless—odd animals, a China plate, an imagined town, a treatise on the growing of camellias. There are no more portraits of literary critics or verse-essays about what poetry should be. The concern is for personal things, deeply felt, imaginatively grasped. The style, again, is in keeping with the content. It becomes ample, slower-moving, and employs metaphors not for their wit but for their power to evoke the visions of an inward place. The grey world of the early thirties simply is not there. Miss Moore has gone inside and closed the door and has furnished her poetry with subjects either timeless or imagined.

The Pangolin and Other Verse gives evidence of a return to the outside world. *What Are Years,* published in 1941 and including the poems from *The Pangolin,* is a collection in which the contemporary world is eminently present. War and threats of war were unavoidably foremost in the minds of everyone in the years between 1935 and 1941. Man lived in a dangerous world. The emotional threats, the metaphysical dangers that haunted Miss Moore's earlier poems are now objectified in the reality of a world on the edge of war. The reality of the danger seems to have made the means of protection more explicit. Where danger was amorphous, aloofness and reticence served as protection. The armoring recommended in the poems of the forties is no longer withdrawal into an inexplicit and rather aristocratic reticence. It is, instead, an inward armoring of self which includes the courage to participate actively in the affairs of man.

As is evident in "The Pangolin," man, himself, in all his confused imperfection becomes an object of sympathy. The scorn of the earlier poems has disappeared. The tone of scolding and judging is gone. In place of these things is understanding and hope. In *What Are Years* and, again, in the 1944 volume, *Nevertheless,* man's moral possibilities create a foundation for hopes, a basis upon which to build his own salvation.

The style of the poems of the forties is much less intricate than is the early poetry. The diction is direct and straightforward with almost none of the Latinate inversion of the early work. The juxtaposing of unlikely images that was the very system of progression in such a poem as "Marriage" becomes less abrupt and, thus, the poems are "easier," more directly accessible. Arbitrary breaking of words to accommodate syllabic count or rhyme-scheme is rare. The overall effect is one of quiet reasoning as though the reader were asked to meditate upon such a question as "What Are Years?" The outside world replaces the inner world in content and the form follows.

The quiet stylistic fireworks of many of the earlier poems are in harmony with subjects primarily visual. A particular object, visually grasped and reported on in visual imagery is the typical poem before 1940. The "meaning" of the poem develops out of images and allusions to a definite object. Generalizations are rare. In the poems written after those included in the *Selected Poems*, the subject may be, occasionally, not a thing but an idea. It may be an abstraction that is bodied forth in specific detail rather than a specific object from which abstractions may be deduced. An uncomplicated style is exactly right for the contemplative content of such poems. This kind of poem is not written to be grasped by intuitive leaps from image to image, but is written to be understood as one understands the thoughtful musings of a friend.

Always one should bear in mind that generalizations about poetic development serve only to suggest overall trends. In any volume of Miss Moore's poems many examples can be found to which the generalizations do not apply. In the *Selected Poems* there are poems which have abstract ideas as subject. In *What Are Years,* there are poems that develop from the observation of a central object. The changes that occur do not, like the advent of the latest Paris fashions, completely wipe out their predecessors. Miss Moore's devotion to the particular object as starting point continues to be evident in all her later poetry. Her use of startling imagery and oddly juxtaposed metaphor never disappears for long. Change in Miss Moore's poetry amounts to addition of new to old rather than replacement of the one by the other. To generalize about trends is really to remark additions.

"What Are Years?" the title poem of the volume, is one of Miss Moore's own favorites. She thinks it is solid, perhaps best written of all her works. It is beautifully written, combining the meticulous finish that one has come to expect of her with intense feeling. The poem soars on the strength of feeling that underlies its precisely constructed exterior. It accomplishes that infrequent feat that seems partly a miracle, embodying in the very texture of the lines the strength and joy of which the poem speaks.

The poem's title poses the questions that have always troubled man: What are years? What is life? What is the point of it all and how best to cope with what never can be really comprehended? All men are naked, "none is safe." Here again is the theme of danger inherent in the life of man against which, as we have seen in "The Pangolin," there is no easy protection. Courage, an inward hardening of the spirit to adversity, is man's best and only protection.

Man is trapped in his own mortality. Struggle as he may, in the end he always loses. His only hope of freedom is, paradoxically, to accept his human predicament, "He / sees deep and is glad, who / accedes to mortality." This acceptance brings a kind of freedom and, in its wake, joy. Only by surrendering do we retain. Only by mastering despair do we experience joy.

Some of the lines in this poem might have come from a hymnal:

> The very bird,
>   grown taller as he sings, steels
> his form straight up. Though he is captive,
> his mighty singing
> says, satisfaction is a lowly
> thing, how pure a thing is joy.

The problem of the poem is the traditional Christian problem, but the suggested solution is not. Had the lines come from a hymnal the strength to withstand and the joy in that strength would have come from God. In Miss Moore's poem they come from within man himself:

> and in his imprisonment rises
> upon himself as
> the sea in a chasm, struggling to be
> free and unable to be,
>   in its surrendering
>   finds its continuing.

The analogy to the sea rising upon itself recalls a similar image in "Sojourn in the Whale" in which eventual freedom for Ireland or for woman was likened to water rising despite obstacles. A simpler freedom was being described. Ireland might, indeed, rise against England, woman against the traditions that held her down, and expect success. Man struggling against the limitations of the human condition can hope for no such ultimate victory. Death is the sooner-or-later reality. To deny it is to deny a part of life. To accept it as a part of being is to affirm life and to find joy.

"Spenser's Ireland" is about people who do not accept and accede to the conditions of life. Instead, they live by superstition, seeking protection in arcane practices, refusing to look at the "rock crystal thing to see." They are stubborn without wisdom, tenaciously clinging to unexamined beliefs:

whoever again
and again says, "I'll never give in," never sees

that you're not free
 until you've been made captive by
 supreme belief—credulity

"Supreme belief" might be interpreted as having a religious significance, but I think that that would be reading too much into the poem. I prefer to think that supreme belief in this poem means something more like the stubborn courage of "What Are Years?" Man is free, not when he tries to avoid danger by black magic, but when he acknowledges his captivity. The supreme belief is the belief in one's own ability to endure unassisted.

Miss Moore is a religious woman. Her upbringing was, of course, traditionally Presbyterian. She thinks that she reads the Bible every day and that she has never really departed from Christian doctrine. Still, traditional Christian doctrine is not clearly apparent in her poetry. Religious faith may underlie all she says about man's peril and the need to seek help within himself, but trust in God for protection and comfort is not mentioned in the poems. Man on his own, self-sustaining, is the figure that emerges from the poetry.

Traditional Christian ethics *are* evident. The qualities of character Miss Moore chooses to admire conform to basic Christian precepts. One gathers from the poetry that Miss Moore's religion involves an adherence to the spirit of Christianity and the practical application of its values to living without necessarily including belief in the efficacy or even existence of God. Man seems advised to practice the Christian virtues but to rely on himself for help and protection. Thus it seems unlikely that "Supreme belief" should be taken to mean belief in God. Rather, I think, we must assume that Miss Moore is talking about a belief in life, an affirmation of life that includes an acceptance, not avoidance, of its perils.

The ostrich of "He 'Digesteth Harde Yron' " is another example of an armored creature but this time toughened from within rather than shielded by shell or scale. He has the inner strength that Miss Moore prizes and that is not always recognized by "the externalist." His courage has grown, fed on the "harde yron" of his existence, until it protects him like an unseen inner shield. She remarks "The power of the visible / is the invisible." (This line was once misprinted, "The power of the invisible is the invisible" to Miss Moore's combined irritation and amusement. She thought the misprint sounded like a parody of the hair-splitting distinctions that abound in her poetry.)

The poem is in a way a paradigm of Miss Moore's poetry. It could be used to illustrate a number of characteristics that are considered typical. The title comes from Lyly's *Euphues:* "The estrich digesteth harde yron to preserve his health." The poem progresses by allusions to and information about ostriches garnered from esoteric books. The form is vaguely syllabic. The rhyming is complicated and eccentric. A particular creature is the subject of the poem and his special characteristics, contrasted with some of the less savory characteristics of man, imply a thesis. A single thoughtful statement is imbedded in the second to last stanza as though it was another object for inspection not unlike the "six hundred ostrich brains served / at one banquet" or an ostrich egg goblet.

The poem never strays far from consideration of its subject and the cruel uses man has made of him and yet the reader senses that the courage of the beleaguered ostrich is meant to have wider application. In the heroism of the ostrich there is a lesson in endurance for man that is about the same as that stated explicitly in "What Are Years?"

The two poems have the same "meaning" but are radically different. The techniques are, of course, strikingly dissimilar, the one depending upon implication, the other upon direct statement to make the same point. The ostrich poem is more like the earlier poetry, in feeling as well as technique. The dominant feelings are approval and disdain, and the meaning derives from an alternation of praise and blame. "What Are Years?" is both more direct in statement and more definitely emotional. The intensity of feeling comes partly from the emotional charge of the language used, partly from the sense of a swelling crescendo in the center lines of each stanza that diminishes again into a final, somehow resigned and melancholy, two-line coda. The rhythm of the stanzas re-capitulates the striving and resigning the poem describes.

The stanzas of "He 'Digesteth Harde Yron' " were originally eight lines long, were compressed to seven in the *Collected Poems* and appear in the *Complete Poems* as a random group of seven-, six- and, once, five-line stanzas. The fewer longer lines contribute to slower movement so that the final version, while sacrificing perfect syllabic count, moves at a more graceful meditative pace. Somehow this revision to longer lines also gives the final version a more emotional quality.

What Are Years contains the poem, "The Student," originally part of the three-part poem, "Part of a Novel, Part of a Poem, Part of a Play," but not printed with the two other portions in the *Selected Poems*. The poem seems to belong to the earlier collection. It speaks of the student as a kind of hero, reclusive and individualistic. Like "The Frigate Pelican" he is uncon-fiding; like Handel in that poem things seem not to touch him, "not because he / has no feeling but because he has so much."

The poem's themes of withdrawal and restraint would seem to tie it to earlier work even without knowledge of its origin. There is a fine difference between the control of the student and the hero and the indomitable endurance of the ostrich. Withdrawal suggests passivity while digesting harde yron to preserve one's health implies meeting life head-on and wresting some kind of accommodation from the struggle. Increasingly in the poetry this need for positive action will be seen until, in "Nevertheless," Miss Moore will say, "Victory won't come / to me unless I go / to it." This is an approach to living quite different from the diffidence suggested by the lines, "The staff, the bag, the feigned inconsequence / of manner, best bespeak that weapon, self-protectiveness."

"The Rigorists" and "Virginia Brittania" are two of Miss Moore's better-known poems, but in neither of them do I find as much to like as in many of those that are less well-known. "The Rigorists" are Alaskan reindeer, well-adapted to the hardships of their region. The poem describes them and ends by saying that their importation to Alaska was a salvation to the Alaskan economy. Their sturdy endurance is, of course, the point. The poem is about as simple as Miss Moore's poems ever get. There are some nice things. The rhyming is subtle and interesting, including both end rhyme and internal rhyme. The reindeer is delightfully described as "this candelabrum-headed ornament / for a place where ornaments are scarce." The final stanza has a kind of sing-song mock innocence that is amusing. But the poem is not one of the wonderful ones in which every detail crisscrosses, underscores, and overlaps until the poem rests in the mind with an existence as real as a day in one's life.

"Virginia Brittania" is a beautiful poem, a lovely evocation in depth of a particular place, but it lacks a center. It occasionally becomes lost in the maze of itself. There is too much going on. There are Indians, Englishmen, both early settlers and more luxurious later residents, and slaves. There are several kinds of trees, native and imported, half a dozen kinds of flowers, birds, snakes, frogs, architecture, furniture, food, clothes, pottery, garden ornaments, a serpentine well, bits of history, bits of botany and economics, all compressed into twelve longish stanzas. The attempt has been to give a composite picture of Virginia including what is native and what imported, a little of its history and a description of its physical characteristics and to make the point in the final stanza that this amalgam has become a new thing, neither as it was originally nor transformed completely by importation, but an indivisible mixture of the two.

The technique is one of superimposition. The poem reminds me of a collage just as, thought of in the span of its history, Virginia might remind one of a collage, new superimposed on old over and over. The technique is admirably suited to the poem's content, and perhaps some confusion is unavoidable. I think part of the confusion comes from allusions tucked into the poem that *are* avoidable. The following lines, for example, are so full of a number of strange things that one's attention flies off in several directions and ends, not in synthesis, but in confusion:

> We-re-wo-
>   co-mo-co's fur crown could be no
>   odder than we were, with ostrich, Latin motto,
> and small gold horseshoe:
>   arms for an able sting-ray-hampered pioneer—
>   painted as a Turk, it seems—continuously
>   exciting Captain Smith

The Notes tell us that Werewocomoco was Powhatan's capital, that Captain Smith had an ostrich, gold horseshoe, and Latin motto in his coat of arms. The allusions to a stingray and a Turk are doubtless also relevant and explainable, but by the time one has gone in confusion to the Notes, one's imagination has been diverted into several channels. All of these details serve, not to concentrate the mind on what the poem is discussing, but, because of their obscurity, to send it off on tangents. An ostrich, a horseshoe, a sting-ray, and a Turk—when their meaning is abstracted from the context—awake

too many irrelevant associations. The cumulative impact of
the lines is lost.

Similarly, lines such as "this little hedge- / sparrow that
wakes up seven minutes sooner than the lark," simply dis-
tract. A little gratuitous information makes one chuckle, but
it doesn't do anything for the poem. And again, the "mag-
nolia's velvet- / textured flower is filled / with anesthetic
scent as inconsiderate as / the gardenia's" is an interesting,
even striking aside but contributes confusion to the whole.
The final line, "clouds . . . are to the child an intimation
of what glory is," is one of two things: either it is totally
irrelevant or it is completely relevant and I don't understand
it. In either case, I do not know why it is there. It seems
heavy with meaning but I cannot explain it at all.

The poem has beauties that may make up for all confusion.
It would be hard to improve on the first stanza. The rhythm
has real elegance. It moves with a calm and stately flow,
long words and long sounds alternating irregularly with shorter
words so that while the progression is slow it is not dull. The
lines, "known to the redbird, the red-coated musketeer, /
the trumpet flower, the cavalier, / the parson, and the wild
parishioner," are held in the parenthesis of "The air is soft,
warm, hot / above the cedar-dotted emerald shore" and "A
deer- / track in a church-floor / brick." Elegance is the
only word for it. It is a Rolls-Royce among rhythms.

There are lovely images throughout the poem. A white
wall-rose has "blunt alternating ostrich-skin warts that were
thorns." There are "cemetery lace settees." Pansies are "fur-
eyed." And there is "the caraway seed- / spotted sparrow
perched in the dew-drenched juniper" in which both the
image and the nervous-bird quality of the word sounds is
striking.

"Light is Speech" is the poem in this volume most directly
concerned with the world situation in 1941. France and her
tradition of free speech and open dissent are the subject.
In 1941, France had been conquered by the Nazis, who occupied the northern and western parts of the country. The

southern and central portions were being ruled by the Vichy government, German-directed.

Light in the sense of enlightenment is the property of speech as much as it is the property of the sun and moon. Voltaire, Montaigne, and Littré defended the right to enlightenment against opposition. This French tradition of light through free speech must, Miss Moore seems to say, be defended still, despite Nazi occupation, despite the treachery of some Frenchmen.

" 'Tell me the truth, / especially when it is / unpleasant' " is a quotation of Marshal Pétain, head of the Vichy government and commonly considered a traitor by the Free French. The lines are ambiguous as they are used here and, I think we must assume, are meant to be ironic. The last lines of the poem would seem to suggest that in spite of these Frenchmen like Pétain who have subverted truth, the French tradition of light in speech remains.

"Light is Speech" is atypical in the body of Miss Moore's work. Seldom is she so outspokenly concerned with world affairs. However, during the 1940s there were several poems that spoke directly and with anguish about the situation man had created for himself. Her well-known "In Distrust of Merits" is one example. "Keeping Their World Large" is another. "Light is Speech" is, by comparison to these, reasoned and controlled. An emotional climate, however, can be felt in a number of the poems of the forties, those dealing only indirectly or not at all with war. There is a feeling of compassion for human beings that is new.

In "The Pangolin," we saw first evidence of this sympathetic concern, not unlike the concern of a mother for a backward child.

> The prey of fear, he, always
> curtailed, extinguished, thwarted by the dusk, work
> partly done,
> says to the alternating blaze,
> "Again the sun!
> anew each day

And yet, "few creatures . . . can make one / breathe faster and make one erecter." "What Are Years?" speaks almost lovingly of threatened, naked man who has the heartbreaking power to sing with joy in his captivity. "Bird-Witted" is all tenderness. The mother bird of the poem, acting instinctively, feeds and protects her fledglings by sheer determination. She is courageous because she has to be; her life demands it. The bird's mothering of the innocent is instinct, but it looks like love. "The Paper Nautilus," too, protects her young by a thin shell which she guards day and night, scarcely eating until her eggs are hatched. Instinct again, but we are told of the shell,

> round which the arms had
> wound themselves as if they knew love
> is the only fortress
> strong enough to trust to.

This is a giant step away from the feigned inconsequence of manner which was the weapon, self-protection, in the early poem. Love, not withdrawal, is the fortress which will protect.

More than half the poems in *What Are Years* are concerned with means of protection. Two poems, "The Student" and "Smooth Gnarled Crape Myrtle," favor reticence and withdrawal. Four or five more are concerned with the development of inner strength, the courage to endure. Two suggest love as protection. The movement has been from passive resistance through a developing courage to an acknowledgment of interdependence.

"Smooth Gnarled Crape Myrtle" is an interesting half-way house in this developing philosophy. The single cardinal who prefers loneliness to the greater loneliness of being with others is like the frigate pelican, perhaps like Miss Moore herself, more comfortable in isolation. There are, however, wistful allusions to the possibility of something else:

> And what of
> our clasped hands that swear, "By Peace

> Plenty; as
> by Wisdom Peace." Alas!

The decoration on a Battersea box, two lovers and the motto, " 'Joined in friendship, crowned by love,' " is another example in contrast to the solitary bird.

"Art is unfortunate" says Miss Moore. "An aspect may deceive," apparently meaning that the isolation of the bird is truer to life than the scene painted on the box. And yet the possibility of something besides loneliness—the clasped hands that swear their motto—is observed with a sigh. The poem ends, "Alas!"

Love, then, is the ultimate fortress, but isolation may be the condition of one's life. In any case inner strength remains essential. This is the thesis of "Nevertheless." It is the first poem in a tiny volume containing only six poems, published in 1944 and called by the name of the title poem. The poem was originally called, "It is Late, I Can Wait," but with the new title it seems a continuation and qualification of the theme of "The Paper Nautilus."

Marguerite Young in her reminiscence, "An Afternoon with Marianne Moore," speaks of the genesis of "Nevertheless." Miss Moore found one day, in a box of strawberries, a flattened green one, almost all seeds. "Here's a strawberry that's had quite a struggle," she said, and used the line with modifications as the first lines of the poem.

"The Paper Nautilus," the last poem in *What Are Years,* ended with the thought that love was "the only fortress strong enough to trust to." The new volume opens on a note of wariness—"Nevertheless [the title here being part of the first line] / you've seen a strawberry / that's had a struggle"—and continues by mentioning the determination to survive that can be noticed in a variety of plants. It is energetic will to succeed that produces success. "Victory won't come / to me unless I go / to it" and

> The weak overcomes its
> menace, the strong over-
> comes itself. What is there

> like fortitude! What sap
> went through that little thread
> to make the cherry red!

In 1944, Marianne Moore was fifty-seven years old. One can only wonder what events in her life influenced her changing feelings. The shy girl in need of mothering who wrote the earliest poems remained, I think, but she had grown tougher and wiser with the years. One thinks of the caustic wit and technical cleverness of the poems in *Observations,* realizing that these stratagems were partly the bravado gestures of a young woman's timidity. The opening to feeling, the womanly tenderness of the early 1940s must have signified a growing confidence, the courage to love and trust. What, then, happened to explain the returning caution of "Nevertheless"? We are unlikely ever to know. It is as though Miss Moore had put a toe into an element that proved too dangerous after all and had chosen to withdraw again, finding caution the better part of wisdom. The shy girl who found safety in diffidence has become the cautious woman who finds, ultimately, no sanctuary but in her own strength.

For Miss Moore wisdom is always that attitude which promises safety. In these poems of the middle 1940s wisdom lies in doubt, independence and willing abandonment. "Elephants" is a poem of abandoned hopes. The elephant is:

> . . . a life prisoner but reconciled.
> With trunk tucked up compactly—the elephant's
> sign of defeat—he resisted, but is the child
>
> of reason now. His straight trunk seems to say: when
> what we hoped for came to nothing, we revived.

He is "the Socrates of animals" because loss cannot alter his tranquillity. He has "contrived" equanimity.

The elephant is the slave to a man he easily might trample. His loss of freedom is at least partly voluntary as perhaps any loss is partly voluntary. We choose what we will sacrifice. The mahout who rests against the elephant although "a defenseless human being" feels as safe as if he, too, were "invincibly tusked, made safe by magic hairs." Thus, in imitating the elephant's gentle resignation, the defenseless human thing has at least the illusion of safety.

The poem seems finally to say that safety comes through a willingness to do without. Like the hero who "covets nothing that it has let go," the elephants revive when their hopes have come to nothing and man, too, may find safety in giving up without resistance whatever it was he had hoped for.

The independence implied in "Elephants," the needing nothing and bearing loss, reaffirms the individualism of "Nevertheless." Loving and trusting others may be well enough but ultimate safety comes from needing nothing but oneself. Loving, or depending on love, must of necessity leave one vulnerable. Dependence can be a threat as well as a comfort, if one fears the withdrawal of the ones depended upon. A protection against being abandoned is to abandon first, and this, it seems to me, is a constant theme in Miss Moore's poetry. Her armored animals, her concern for reticence, her insistence on self-sufficiency, her distrust of all safe harbors outside herself seem defenses against the ultimate danger of loving what may not endure.

The elephant's wisdom comes partly from his willingness to bear loss. It comes, too, from his peaceful acceptance of uncertainty. As Socrates knew that "the wisest is he who's not sure that he knows," so the elephant knows he must contrive equanimity in the face of uncertainty. Loss, uncertainty, broken hopes—these are the conditions of life with which man tries to deal. His usual means are through religion or love or intellectuality. In Miss Moore's stoic world of frightened creatures, religion, love and even knowledge are untrustworthy tigers to ride. Where security is an absolute necessity only the surest means of protection will suffice. Thus, "Who rides on a tiger can never dismount; / asleep on an elephant, that is repose."

One of the really interesting poems in *Nevertheless* is called "The Mind is An Enchanting Thing." Miss Moore described the inspiration for this poem as coming when the phrase "katydid-wing / subdivided by sun / till the nettings are legion" sprang into her mind. This is how most poems start for her, she thinks, with a "felicitous phrase" that occurs simultaneously "with some thought or object of equal attraction." Partly it was the light, inconspicuous rhyme that attracted her to this phrase, and, from the intricacy suggested by the image, she wove a description of the intricacy of the mind.

The mind, at once enchanting and enchanted, is described first by images that stress complexity: the nettings of a katydid wing, the intricacies of Scarlatti. It feels rather than sees its way. It hears with memory's ear. It has a certainty within itself not dependent on outside things. "It is a power of / strong enchantment."

This is certainly not the conscious, rational mind Miss Moore is describing. It is instead the iridescent mind of the imagination that deals in "conscientious inconsistency" and sees beneath the veils and romantic delusions the rational mind sets up.

"Unconfusion submits / its confusion to proof; it's / not a Herod's oath that cannot change." The certainties of reason, all confusion really, are sorted by this imaginative mind which, unlike its rational counterpart, does not insist on certainty. Inconsistency is the true unconfusion the poem seems to say. It is the enchanted source of creation.

One of the pleasures of this poem is its weaving of several single words through the poem's length with a subtle varying of meaning. The word "eye" for example is first the eye of the mind, then the eye of the memory, then the eye of the heart, suggesting three ways of "seeing" that do not involve sight, but insight. Sun makes apparent the netting of the katydid's wing, the iridescence of the dove-neck, unseen things made visible. Iridescence of wing and neck, inconsistency of mind and music are all enchanted and somehow interwoven. The poem is a picture of something invisible made visible by the strong light, the intuitive eye, of the power of imagination that is also the poem's subject.

"In Distrust of Merits" is possibly Miss Moore's best known

poem. It is the one that turns up most often in anthologies and is quoted frequently because, sadly, it has been pertinent for most of the last twenty years. Miss Moore has said that she would not call it a poem. "It's truthful; it is testimony— to the fact that war is intolerable, and unjust." But she feels that because its form is haphazard, disjointed, exclamatory, it is not a poem. "It is just a protest. . . . Emotion overpowered me. First this thought and then that."

It would be unfortunate should she be popularly known primarily on the strength of this poem because it is not nearly of the quality of the great body of her work. The intricacy and precision that ordinarily inform her poetry are not so evident here and neither is the honesty. Curiously, this most popular of her poems is perhaps least Marianne Moore-like. It is easy to understand. The emotion and the ideas are all surface and, for these reasons, it is probably easiest to like for those who think reading poetry should require no more effort than taking a bath.

How this poem might have been written is understandable. War *is* horrible, horrible to take part in and horrible to contemplate. Bewildered emotion is appropriate and possibly does much to explain the uncharacteristic banality of the poem's conclusion:

> There never was a war that was
>   not inward; I must
> fight till I have conquered in myself what
> causes war, but I would not believe it.
>   I inwardly did nothing.
>   O Iscariot-like crime!

Miss Moore is here only repeating one of the clichés about war.

Randall Jarrell found objectionable the idea that "if these great patient / dyings—all these agonies / and wound bearings and bloodshed— / can teach us how to live, these / dyings were not wasted," and so do I. Again, this is the last-resort cliché of a person desperate to find some comfortable way to look at what is impossible to look at. But the possible enlightenment is not worth the price of the lesson and to say it is is silly.

For me there is something unpleasant in Miss Moore's concern for her own guilt in this poem. Her characteristic modesty would, here, have been welcome. Her own agony of guilt, coupled with the simplistic statements about hatred and personal responsibility, are irritating, juxtaposed to the real agonies of dying in the poem. The effect, I think, is of an unattractively narrowed concern, but the poem interests me as it fits with the other poems of the period.

Most of Miss Moore's poetry is self-centered as, perhaps, all poetry is and has to be. Peculiar to Miss Moore's self-concern, however, is its emphasis on self-protection with concomitant non-involvement and withdrawal. Her concern for others has nearly always been in terms of identification with their vulnerability which, finally, begins to seem more like care for a projected self than real concern for real people. It is possible, then, that the guilt Miss Moore expresses in this poem comes from an acknowledgment of the cowardice of deliberate non-involvement. She has, indeed, inwardly done nothing or, more accurately, has deliberately set out to avoid being involved. Whether there is any validity in the idea of morally involving oneself is a separate question. The point is that for Miss Moore to feel this particular guilt is interesting in light of the persistent theme of a great deal of her poetry.

"In Distrust of Merits" is one of the two poems Miss Moore has ever written that can be criticized for being trite. The other is also a war poem, "Keeping Their World Large." Always her ideas are original and their expression is unique, with these two exceptions. Here, clichés are used to substitute for feeling. When one's own feelings are not strong enough, one borrows another man's words; strong feelings dictate their own vocabulary.

I think there is a curious lack of feeling in "In Distrust of Merits." It is as though Miss Moore had felt constrained to write a poem about war and had tried to crank out appropriate emotions. There is something very like cranking in the triple repetitions of the word *fighting* and in the melodra-matic *O's*. These rhetorical devices simply don't occur in other poems. Lines like "We / vow, we make this promise / to the fighting—it's a promise—'We'll / never hate black, white, red, yellow, Jew / Gentile, Untouchable'" are so frantically insistent that the style begins to seem like a retraction of the content. If you really mean it, you don't have to promise three times. At least two of those promises are meant to convince the poet herself she really means it.

CHAPTER VIII 〜 FABLES AND COLLECTED POEMS

〜 WITH PUBLICATION of the two volumes of the 1940s, Miss Moore began to win prizes and recognition on every hand. In 1940, she had won the Shelley Memorial Award. In 1944 she won both the Harriet Monroe Poetry Award and the Contemporary Poetry's Patrons' Prize. In 1945, she was awarded a Guggenheim Fellowship and, in 1946, a joint grant from the National Institute of Arts and Letters and the American Academy of Arts and Letters.

During these years she occasionally worked in areas other than her own poetry. In 1945, she translated a Christmas story from Adalbert Stifter's *Bunte Steine* in collaboration with Elizabeth Mayor, calling it *Rock Crystal*. The story is of two children who lose their way in the Alps on Christmas Eve but are saved by a vision. The style is practically glacial. The children are stick figures, but the work is interesting as a tour de force of glittering intricacy.

In 1942, Miss Moore taught composition for a time at Cummington School in Massachusetts, as a visiting lecturer. Subsequently she was visiting lecturer at poetry seminars, readings and the like at such diverse schools as Harvard, Vassar, and the University of California.

In 1946, she set to work on a translation of the *Fables of La Fontaine*. The translations took eight years and were rewritten four times. Her original interest in La Fontaine, she says, was entirely independent of the content of the fables.

She was apparently attracted to his rhythm and rhyming. One can see, in comparing her translations to the French, that she is much more scrupulous about reproducing his unaccented line and near-rhyme than she is about literally translating the words and images. The form of La Fontaine's stanzas is mirror-imaged in the translations, but the style of description is characteristic Marianne Moore.

Next, she says, she "fell a prey to that surgical kind of courtesy of his,"[1] and small wonder. In this area she and La Fontaine are kindred spirits. The La Fontaine passage she quotes as an example of "surgical courtesy" would be perfectly at home in any of her own poems:

> I fear that appearances are worshiped throughout France
> Whereas pre-eminence perchance
> Merely means a pushing person.

W. H. Auden suggested Miss Moore as a possible translator to a publisher in 1945 and the publisher subsequently commissioned her to do the *Fables*. After she was well into the work the publisher who had commissioned the translations died and she was left feeling that his company might rather not continue the project. She worked on for awhile but felt that it was not going well. One can imagine the difficulty of the work, given Miss Moore's drive for perfection and her limited grasp of French, for, while she had some French, it would be inaccurate to say she knew the language well.

Eventually she decided to volunteer to break her contract so that she could offer the translations to another publisher. Macmillan had taken an interest in her work and she submitted the parts that she had finished to the editor in charge of translations there. This was in January. She remembers that she had "a kind of uneasy hope that all would be well." In the meantime there were volumes left to translate, "hours, and years of work," and, hoping for a favorable response from Macmillan, she set about finishing the job that remained.

Miss Moore remembers that, in May, Macmillan's editor responded: "Well, I studied French at Cornell, took a degree in French, I love French, and . . . well, I think you'd better put it away for a while." Miss Moore says that she asked for how long, and the editor replied, "About ten years; besides, it will hurt your own work. You won't write so well afterward."

Miss Moore had felt that the translations would benefit her own work and had undertaken them partly for that reason. Years later she still thinks that they were the best help she has ever had, training her ear, giving her, at that time, "momentum." She argued with the editor's objections, asked, "What is wrong? Have I not a good ear? Are the meanings not sound?"

"Well, there are conflicts," the editor replied, and repeated it, Miss Moore says, countless times. She has no idea what the conflicts might have been, but she asked the editor simply to return the material. Miss Moore confesses to having been desperate at this rejection. She had worked four years on the translations and was at a loss to know where she had gone wrong and what she might do to salvage some part of her labor.

Finally she decided to ask for help from Ezra Pound. She has always been reluctant to ask for assistance with her work except from perhaps "a librarian or someone whose business it was to help applicants." She told Charles Norman, Ezra Pound's biographer, that although she boasted of never having asked for help, in this case she was "feeling fit and ready to die"[2] and sent Pound several of the *Fables* and a letter saying, "The editor in charge feels that I had better put the material away for a few years (I think he said ten) . . . I infer that my ear is not good. Will you take time to tell me if the rhythms grate on you?" The request for help was sent to Pound at St. Elizabeth's Hospital in Washington, where he was living through years of unhappiness and disgrace. One wonders whether Miss Moore, in seeking his help, was not inadvertently conferring a greater favor on Pound than any she was asking of him.

At any rate Pound replied: "Yes, m'dr Marianna the least taint of quality an / or merit upsets these blighters. Lez see the rest of 'em." He suggested she try Faber or some other

London publisher. In another letter he offered to try having them printed in one of the few periodicals he read. A year later he again wrote, saying that he would be glad to help but could not concentrate, then suggested she "KICK OUT this god damned french syntax, with relative clauses. WRITE the sense in plain english, PROSE, and then versify the SENSE of your prose." Miss Moore remarked, "He was very severe with me."

She and Pound had admired one another for years, Pound being one of the earliest poets to recognize her talent, she recognizing Pound's greatness as early as his 1910 *Spirit of Romance*. They had corresponded for two decades before they met. On Pound's visit to the United States in 1939 he called Miss Moore in Brooklyn one evening, saying that he would come for supper. He wanted eggs and cold cuts at her apartment. She took him to supper at a nearby restaurant. She walked him to the subway afterwards, commented that T. S. Eliot's brother, Henry, whom she liked and admired and whom Pound did not know, was "more the artist than anyone I've ever met." Pound turned to her. "Now, now, be careful," he said.

Pound had intended to make a second visit to Brooklyn but he never did. He and Miss Moore did not meet again until she went to visit him in St. Elizabeth's. She went several times, bringing candy for him and peanuts for the bluejays and squirrels on the hospital grounds. An official escorting her through the grounds once remarked, "Good of you to come to see him," to which she replied, "Good? You have no idea how much he has done for me, and others." Perhaps she was thinking in particular of the encouragement Pound had given her in her bewilderment over the *Fables*.

At about the same time, Monroe Engel of the Viking Press asked to look at the *Fables* if Miss Moore had no other commitment. She was enormously relieved and grateful but replied, "I can't offer you something which somebody else thinks isn't fit to print. I would have to have someone to stabilize it and guarantee that the meanings are sound." Engel concurred and asked whom she would like to have undertake the job. She chose Harry Levin at Harvard, she says, because she had admired his review of Edna St. Vincent Millay's and George Dillon's translation of Baudelaire. (Professor Levin actually never reviewed these translations. Miss Moore must have been thinking of another reviewer. But the error was pure serendipity.) She insisted on offering him money from what would have been her advance against royalties, declining to take anything in advance for herself. Levin refused the money but accepted the task as a "refreshment against the chores of the term" and undertook the job with a precision and kindness that delighted Miss Moore.

Levin has written an essay called "A Note on Her French Aspect" in which he speaks of Miss Moore's affinity for certain French modes of thought and expression. He says:

In practical terms, this direction has led to the most remarkable of her technical accomplishments, the use of syllabic versification in English. Its monument comprises the varied yet faithful stanzas of her exquisite translation of La Fontaine's *Fables*, where the human bestiary has been so thoroughly assimilated that the *esprit gaulois* is refined into a quintessence of Yankee wit.[3]

In many ways Marianne Moore and La Fontaine display such striking similarities in their respective verse that the one seems a spiritual descendent of the other. Their styles are remarkably alike. Syllabic versification and light, unaccented rhyme was Miss Moore's customary mode long before she translated La Fontaine. Both have a liking for precision that exhibits itself in the most delicate shadings of language. Both are possessed of a dry wit and a wry view when observing human nature. Animal subjects, what Levin calls the human bestiary, are, of course, common to the poetry of both. The "surgical courtesy" Miss Moore admires in La Fontaine is equally apparent in her own work and bespeaks a philosophy of living as much as a style of expression. Finally, they share an ethical code. The morals of La Fontaine's *Fables* would be wholly congenial to Miss Moore's view of things and, in fact, many of the human values implied in the *Fables* have been more-or-less plainly expressed in her poetry.

For all the similarities, there is at least one major difference between the poetry of Marianne Moore and that of La Fontaine, and it is strikingly evident in the translations. Miss Moore is a poet of the eye first, a poet of the intellect second. La Fontaine is brain first and imagistic only occasionally. His *Fables* are prose written in verse. Miss Moore, on the other hand, does verbal water colors. She has transformed the *Fables,* in translating them, from black and white to bright colors. She has brought metaphor into the translations wherever she can do so without sacrificing the sense of a passage. She is scrupulously careful to imitate La Fontaine's versification but often transforms a line with her own metaphor.

Any number of La Fontaine's lines could be compared to Miss Moore's translations of them to illustrate what she has done. From the fable, "The Fox and The Grapes" for example, Miss Moore translates the lines:

> Des raisins mûrs apparemment
> Et couverts d'une peau vermeille.[4]

as

> Matured till they glowed with a purplish tint
> As though there were gems inside.

La Fontaine's ripe grapes with vermillion skin have become alive in translation, glowing, mouth-watering, precious and even perhaps a little mysterious, enlivened by the eye of Miss Moore's imagination.

In the fable of "The Fox and the Crow" La Fontaine's fox greets the crow conventionally enough, albeit flatteringly:

> Et bonjour, Monsieur du Corbeau.
> Que vous êtes joli! que vous me semblez beau!

The crow is called pretty, even beautiful in these lines, but in Miss Moore's version he is flattered nearly off his perch by the extravagance of her metaphors:

> Aha, superb Sir Ebony, well met.
> How black! who else boasts your metallic jet!

Which tells you exactly what a crow looks like!

The moral of "The Lion in Love" is made livelier in translation by the addition of a single image. La Fontaine says "Amour, amour, quand tu nous tiens / On peut bien dire: Adieu prudence." Miss Moore translates this: "Love, ah Love, when your slipknot's drawn / We can but say, 'Farewell, good sense.' "

A lion is bitten by a gnat in "The Lion and The Gnat" and he is enraged. La Fontaine's lion foams and his eye throws out sparks. Miss Moore's lion also foams, then lightning shoots from his eyeball. La Fontaine's gnat retires with glory. Miss Moore's withdraws "in a halo of fire."

"The Crow Aping the Eagle" seeks to lift a lamb as he has seen the eagle do. La Fontaine calls the lamb a woolly creature. Miss Moore calls him a "woolly masterpiece in fur." One could continue citing lines endlessly in which Miss Moore has changed simple description to livelier metaphor. Of course, there are a number of *Fables* as well where the translation is close to the wording of the original, as in, "The City Mouse and the Country Mouse." This happens usually in *Fables* where action is rapid and continuous, where La Fontaine has taken time for description himself and has, thus, offered Miss Moore little latitude for using her own imagination.

Translating poetry from one language to another requires a choice. One must decide whether to be faithful to the verse form of the original or to the literal translation of word and image. If one chooses to imitate the rhythm and rhyme scheme, literal translation is impossible and, of course, the converse is also true. In deciding to stay as close as possible to La Fontaine's versification, Miss Moore chose wisely. The strength of La Fontaine's poetry is in its wit and in its elegant versification. These things are preserved in translation. The sacrifice of literal wording turns out not to be a sacrifice at all for Miss Moore brings to her new phrases a fire of visual imagery which is, perhaps, the one thing the original lacks.

The spirit of La Fontaine's *Fables* is intact, and it is maintained by a number of methods. La Fontaine's wit is a delicate thing and derives more often than not from a droll characterization accomplished by the most subtle choice of words. To achieve the same effect in another language would seem nearly impossible given the importance of connotation to humor. Wisely, Miss Moore did not seek verbal equivalents to do the job, but found means of her own to accomplish similar ends. An example is the fable of "The Grasshopper and the Ant." La Fontaine says that the ant is not a lender, using the word, *prêteuse,* which is somehow comic with its human overtones. This, says La Fontaine, was her least fault. Does he mean, then, that not to be a lender was her smallest fault among many larger ones or that it was the fault of which she was least likely to be guilty? Miss Moore has chosen the latter reading, so dispensing with the ambiguity, but has preserved the tiny ant's personality and, thus, the humor, by translating the passage: "Share one's seeds? Now what is worse / For any ant to do?"

Sometimes Miss Moore is drier and funnier than La Fontaine. The final two lines of "The Fox and The Stork" are an example. La Fontaine says, "Trompeurs, c'est pour vous que j 'écris, / Attendez-vous à la pareille." Miss Moore translates the lines thus: "My words here are particularly / Addressed to foxes without fur." In another *Fable,* "The Wolf and The Stork," La Fontaine is funny, but Miss Moore is funnier. The stork demands compensation for having pulled a bone from the wolf's throat. La Fontaine's wolf is a scoundrel. He is amazed she would ask payment, tells her she's joking. Miss Moore's wolf is both scoundrel and wit. " 'Compensate?' he inquired with bared teeth, / 'A humorist, I infer!' "

Then, there are lots of simply pretty things in the translations. The grasshopper of the grasshopper and ant fable "Chose to chirr" and "Chirred a recurrent chant." This is no attempt to imitate word sounds found in La Fontaine, but does seem an attempt to imitate a grasshopper. In La Fontaine the grasshopper sings and cries, *chant* and *crie,* and in neither case does the poet seem to try particularly to imitate a grasshopper's sound.

The words *clopin clopant* appear in La Fontaine's "The

Pot of Clay and the Pot of Iron." The words mean to hobble along and have the sort of sound a hobbling clay pot and a pot of iron might make walking together. Miss Moore translates this, "Clipper-clap-clip they tried their luck," imitating the sound but at the same time suggesting a jauntier pace than La Fontaine apparently intended. Hers are a younger pair of pots, and funnier. (I can't say why.)

Miss Moore characteristically tidies up a line or two from time to time so that her translated version is even more discreet and proper than is La Fontaine's, although he could hardly be called ribald. For example, in "The Oak and the Reed" La Fontaine speaks of a fierce wind as a terrible child that the North had carried in its flanks (these lines, incidentally, being unusually metaphoric for La Fontaine). Miss Moore leaves the flanks out and says, "A fury of destruction / Which the North had nursed in some haunt known to none." The North as mother of the wind is still the image, but she is in a more decorous phase of her motherhood.

So, too, is impending birth slightly spiritualized in Miss Moore's translation of "Bitch and Friend." There is something earthy in La Fontaine's lines, "Une lice étant sur son terme / Et ne sachant où mettre un fardeau si pressant," that is absent in Miss Moore's translation. The dog of the fable is pregnant, full term, and does not know where to put a burden "si pressant," meaning urgent, but also suggesting heavy and pressing in the sense, possibly, of the pressure of birth. Miss Moore's bitch is pregnant, too, but is in a very antiseptic state by comparison: "A bitch who approached each hutch with a frown, / Since a-shiver to shelter an imminent litter." Notice the heavy, slow vowels of the French version that have to be uttered deep in the throat and compare them to the sibilant consonants and short "i's" of Miss Moore's version that virtually hold the whole affair at arm's length.

In her Foreword to the translation Miss Moore thanks several dozen people for help with her work and at the same time denigrates her own ability and accomplishment in her customary manner. She thanks, in particular, Malcolm Cowley, saying that because of his help he should be called "Supervisor Extraordinary of the present version," if so doing would not be a "disservice," crediting him "with what he might repudiate." Cowley had apparently had much to do with checking the accuracy of the translation, had once told Miss Moore that portions of the work were "rather far from the French." Monroe Engel "ameliorated persisting ungainliness." Wallace Fowlie and Robert Franc read certain typical fables aloud in French. Kathrine Jones rectified "an erroneous concept of accent," thus providing "a veritable rescue" for Miss Moore whose effort was to approximate the rhyme of La Fontaine. Fowlie and Franc, thanks to their reading, "obviated purblindnesses of indecision."

Pound is singled out for special thanks. His practices, particularly as regards rhythm and syntax, were, she says, her "governing principle." Pound's "Guido Cavalcanti," his "Seafarer" and some of his French songs were the works from which she deduced the principles of natural word order, active voice, the rejection of dead words and "rhymes synonymous with gusto." Pound, as we have seen, made explicit these same principles in one of his letters to her about the translations.

She thanks her brother, to whom the translations are dedicated, for "fixed confidence on his part in the auspiciousness of my efforts." She mentions the influence on her of her mother's liking for "verbal decorum," says that the influence has led her "to dislike, if not avoid, contractions and the wish for the deed."

Twenty-three of the several hundred translated fables were included in *A Marianne Moore Reader*, published by Viking Press in 1961. The selection was evidently Miss Moore's and can be assumed to include those she thought best or liked best among her translations. I think the group does include most of the best ones. They are, at least, the ones in which Miss Moore's own mark is most evident, including a number of the ones I have just discussed, and they give a good idea of the general style and energy of the hundreds not included. Again in the *Complete Poems* Miss Moore chose a few of the translations for reprinting.

Miss Moore's mother did not live to see the publication of the *Fables*. She died in 1947, shortly after the translations had been begun, and one can only imagine what disruption her death caused in her daughter's life. Certainly they had been unusually close. Miss Moore's admiration for her mother's mind and her reliance upon her mother's critical judgment and encouragement were enormous. Her poetry, when its stoic self-reliance unbends as in "Bird-Witted" or "The Paper Nautilus," speaks specifically of the dependence of a child upon a mother. This first most basic relationship is really as close as Miss Moore comes to love in her poems. Concern for humanity—in such poems as "The Pangolin" and "What Are Years?"—seems to verge on an almost loving tenderness but has really, again, a maternal quality. One realizes that in her concern for unprotected man Miss Moore is both the mothering and the mothered. Deep feeling shows itself in restraint and Miss Moore rarely speaks of her mother's death. When she does mention her it is to talk admiringly of her mind or to speak of something they once did together, to quote a particularly apt phrase, or to remember an especially happy time.

Miss Moore continued to live alone in the apartment in Brooklyn. In 1947, she was elected to the National Institute of Arts and Letters. In 1949, she was awarded the first of many honorary degrees, a Litt. D. from Wilson College. In 1950, Mount Holyoke and Smith conferred honorary degrees on her. In 1951, the honor was from the University of Rochester.

Macmillan brought out a volume of the *Collected Poems* in 1951. The book is dedicated to Miss Moore's mother and contains as the first section the poems of the *Selected Poems* with some revisions. The second and third sections include the poems of *What Are Years* and *Nevertheless,* and there is a fourth section of nine "Hitherto Uncollected" poems. A *Collected Poems* was brought out simultaneously in London by Faber and Faber, publishers of the *Selected Poems*.

Omitted from the 1951 *Collected Poems* are seven poems that had been published in magazines between 1935 and 1951. Four of the omissions date from the late thirties. The three others appeared in the early fifties. They are "We Call Them Brave," a war poem meditating on courage; "Quoting an Also Private Thought" which talks, essentially, about privacy; and "Pretialae." "Pretialae" is impenetrable and, so, of course, fascinating. It is a poem of forty-one words to which are appended about eighty words of notes. As is usually the case with Miss Moore's notes, they don't help much; the poem remains for me an interesting enigma.

Of the nine new poems appended to the *Collected Poems*, all had appeared in magazines after the 1944 publication of "Nevertheless." The poem, "A Face," had been written to fulfill the request of Cyril Connelly who asked Miss Moore for something to publish in his *Horizon*. Miss Moore remembers it as one of the few poems she ever wrote that didn't give her any trouble. It is, perhaps for this reason, a not very interesting poem. Its grammar is peculiar and one believes at first that there must be more there than meets the eye—but I don't think so. Miss Moore looks in a mirror and sees nothing revealing of her character, bad or good. She remembers certain other faces in which character could be read, and they are a delight to think about. There may be a suggestion in the poem of the difficulty one has in knowing himself. There is certainly something piquantly Marianne Moore-like in her concern, not for her coiffure, but for her character.

"By Disposition of Angels" is, I think, about the inexpressible mystery that informs character or poetry with an inner light. As angels are ephemeral and yet have steadfast existence, so, too, is this mystery. How to speak of what is ineffable is the problem of the poem. Mystery can be described only obliquely, as "something heard most clearly when not near it" or as the light of a star becomes apparent only in relation to surrounding darkness. Only "mysteries expound mysteries." The quality of inner light is there like the dazzling light of the star, "live and elate." It does not derive its existence from being articulated. It would, in fact, like a fir tree "not wish me to uproot it," as through digging too deep to explain mystery may have the effect of killing it.

Of course, paraphrasing this poem is like uprooting a fir
tree: in one stomps with muddy boots treading down all
subtlety and nuance in a desperate attempt to yank out
meaning by the roots. It might be better to quote these four
lovely lines and have done with it:

> Star that does not ask me if I see it?
> Fir that would not wish me to uproot it?
> Speech that does not ask me if I hear it?
>   Mysteries expound mysteries.

"The Icosasphere" is a crazy quilt of attributions. It is
like a lot of Miss Moore's later poems in which an item or
several items from a newspaper or other current source are
stitched together with a little irony to make wry comment on
contemporary life. These poems tend toward light verse and,
in general, I like them less than her other poetry although
they are amusing.

Birds nesting in "the merged green density" of Bucking-
hamshire hedgerows weave perfect "parabolic concentric
curves" from the bits of debris they collect. Mr. J. O. Jackson
has brought steel-cutting to "its summit of economy" by
developing some method with twenty conjoined triangles that
will wrap a ball with no waste. Other persons, contesting
their claims to a $30 million snuff fortune, have committed
a variety of atrocities upon themselves and others. The Egyp-
tians built the pyramids. From these scraps Miss Moore fashions a little meditation on human nature and potential in
which the birds in the hedgerows, acting instinctively, come
off best. Human instincts, being more complicated, unfortunately diverge in many directions. Ingenuity and persistence
are only two potentials in human nature. Greed and mayhem
are others, human nature being a twenty-sided whole, an
icosasphere.

In "His Shield" Miss Moore is back to armoring in one of
the most gusto-filled poems on this subject. The first stanza
of the poem is such a wonderful mouthful that there is nothing
but quoting that will do it justice:

The pin-swin or spine-swine
    (the edgehog miscalled hedgehog) with all his edges out,
  echidna and echinoderm in distressed-
pin-cushion thorn-fur coats, the spiny pig or porcupine,
    the rhino with horned snout—
  everything is battle-dressed.

The lines themselves bristle, have sharp-edged sounds. Such extravagant spikiness of sound and image begins to seem a parody of itself and I think there is some self-mockery intended here. As in the line from "The Pangolin," "Another armored animal," in this first stanza of "His Shield" Miss Moore seems to admit a humorous, helpless recognition of her eccentric concern.

Acknowledging one's hang-up does not get rid of it, necessarily, as the rest of "His Shield" makes plain. Presbyter—or Prester—John, dressed in salamander skin that could withstand flame, walked safely through the fires of life. His real shield was his humility. Although he lived in a country where "rubies large as tennis / balls conjoined in streams so / that the mountain seemed to bleed" he was without greed and this was a protection. Like "The Hero," Presbyter John was armored with "the power of relinquishing / what one would keep."

This idea of safety in humility was the theme of "Elephants" as well. Wanting or needing things or people leads, in Miss Moore's world, to captivity. Independence is freedom. But might one not be a prisoner to the need for independence?

Humility, when you think about it, is a shield for rather curious reasons and too much humility is a bore. After all, if one can do something well, what is the point of pretending that one can't? No poor poet ever wrote a stanza like the first one of "His Shield." No bungler could come close to the excellence of the La Fontaine translation. Anybody who can write that way is good and it seems highly doubtful that Miss Moore doesn't know it. Humility is a shield because it seeks to disarm. If you get there first with your own self-criticism you effectively take the wind from the sails of subsequent critics. This is pretty good armor, but it is questionable humility.

Anyone studying Miss Moore's editorship of the *Dial* would have difficulty believing in the genuineness of her humility. She is good and she knows it. How else explain the revisions and changes she insisted upon in the work of others? Humility, then, and "the power of relinquishing what one would keep" do not provide real independence but, instead, simply acknowledge how great is the need to depend. Humility protects by disarming criticism. Relinquishing implies letting go of what is valued before it is snatched away by force. In either case one is so attached to what is threatened that the take-it-or-leave-it attitude of true independence is impossible. The kind of independence that is seen to serve as protection implies real need for that which one is independent from, and in either accepting or fighting against the need, one remains captive to it.

"His Shield" ends with the lines, "be / dull. Don't be envied or / armed with a measuring rod." This is man's best protection according to Miss Moore, but it would be an armor necessary only to those who want, more than anything, to be best. Contrived humility can only bespeak a soul not very humble.

"Keeping Their World Large" is another war poem in which the death of American soldiers is likened to the death of Christ, both sacrifices made so that mankind might live. As in "In Distrust of Merits" I think the emotion of this poem is somewhat contrived. It tends to sentimentality, by definition false feeling, and to clichés, which in Miss Moore's poetry are signals that something is askew. Another minor point that allies this poem to "In Distrust of Merits" is the triple repetition of the word, "marching," connoting, I think, the same kind of straining after intensity that it did in the earlier poem.

The central image of the poem, the comparison of Christ's death to war casualties and the implication of resurrection to be achieved through the abandonment of egocentrism, is sentimental. The mention of Christ's death in this connection serves to lend conventional emotion to a subject to which Miss Moore brings no original feeling. The sacrifice of Isaac is employed to the same end in the poem. Politicians often do this kind of thing, paralleling one situation to another that conventionally carries with it a load of preconceived ideas and predictable emotions. Everytime somebody calls something "another Munich," he is depending on the emotional freight attached to that term to inspire similar emotion for the other term of his analogy.

It is possible that the parallel drawn between Christ's death and the deaths of war could be legitimate, but Miss Moore expresses the analogy in the furriest old clichés and one has to doubt her success in realizing her emotion. I cannot accept lines like, " 'If Christ and the apostles died in vain, I'll / die in vain with them' " as anything but contrived in their feeling. Similarly, "when the very heart was a prayer," "These, laid like animals for sacrifice, / like Isaac on the mount," "clothed in fear," "this sick scene" are all commonplace ideas of more or less venerable age.

But, perhaps most of all, the words themselves are give-aways. Miss Moore is the poet of the freshly laundered phrase and, yet, we find expression like "in vain," "very heart," "forest of white crosses," "tears that don't fall," "fat living and self-pity." All of these phrases belong to someone else, or could. The poet of "fern-seed footprints" is out of sight, hiding herself behind someone else's emotional vocabulary.

I much prefer a poem like "Efforts of Affection" which, although it is practically incomprehensible, is uniquely itself. The poem has something to do with independence and integration, the possibility of a whole containing two independent parts.

It reminds me of "Marriage," in which the same theme appeared in much the same style. Absence of connectives is common to both poems and accounts in large part for the opaqueness of both. The leap from image to image, with no explanation to help the reader leap along, is the technique that inspired Williams to call "Marriage" "an anthology of transit." Williams, too, was the one who assured us that when one finally penetrated to the meaning of one of Miss Moore's poems, the maze of the technique would be seen

as necessary. I take this on faith in "Efforts of Affection."
I believe there is an essential link between Jubal and Jabal—
Shakespeare's sweet hay and an elephant-ear plant—that
someday may come clear to me. In the meantime it is possible to enjoy things like "Vermin-proof and pilfer-proof integration" or "Unsheared sprays of elephant-ears" without
really knowing how they relate to each other. One can, after
all, admire a handful of pretty pebbles.

"Voracities and Verities Sometimes Are Interacting" is
another obscure poem, a little less so than "Efforts of Affection." The leaps are shorter, perhaps. Less flexibility is
required of the reader's imagination. Miss Moore seems to be
saying that aggressive obtrusiveness, like the diamond's, is
unpleasant, better "the emerald's 'grass-lamp glow.'" In one
instance, however, aggressive extravagance is pardonable,
and that is in love. Here truth and appetite interact.

It interests me that in these two poems and in "Marriage,"
three of Miss Moore's most obscure works, the subject is love
—not mothering love, but, one gathers, love between the
sexes. I wonder whether the obliqueness of the method has
anything to do with the subject. The obliqueness is almost
entirely a result of the lack of connectives, as in:

> Genesis tells us of Jubal and Jabal.
> One handled the harp and one herded the cattle.
>
> Unhackneyed Shakespeare's
> "Hay, sweet hay, which hath no fellow."

The obscurity seems to lie entirely in the suppression of the
copula.

"Propriety" is a poem full of pleasant things to say, words
that feel good in the mouth: "near the root of the throat;"
"The fish-spine / on firs, on / somber trees / by the sea's /
walls of wave-worn rock;" "mixed with wits;" "blackened /
because born that way." It is full, too, of things to see: the
bird, "spiraling a tree— / up up up like mercury;" "resistance
with bent head like foxtail / millet's;" and "unintentional
pansy-face." And it is talking about the word, propriety, a

fitness or suitability, which can be seen in the things mentioned and which is described by them. Propriety is demonstrated in "Bach's cheerful firmness," in "a not long / sparrow-song / of hayseed / magnitude— / a tuned reticence with rigor / from strength at the source." The poem, itself, might be an example of propriety in that the form and language are entirely suitable to the subject.

Although the title of the last poem in this volume is "Armor's Undermining Modesty," suggesting immediately the shield of humility, the subject of the poem is, I think, not protection but poetry.

A moth alights on the poet's wrist, seeming at first a pest, but soon seen to be beautiful in its inadvertent intricacy. Immediately the scene shifts to early man hacking out our alphabet with hairy paws. How can one express the delicate moth of a feeling in something as coarse as language, as "mis-set," and imprecise?

"No wonder we hate poetry, / and stars and harps and the new moon." We hate poetry, apparently, because poetry and its "poetic" language do not express the felt truth of our intuition, as perhaps we have expected them to. The only close approach language can make to this intuitive sense is by indirection: "What is more precise than precision? Illusion." And if poetry does not do this, "if tributes cannot / be implicit," then Miss Moore would prefer the strong, aseptic and impersonal—"diatribes and the fragrance of iodine." In short, she would prefer an honest coarseness to a pretense of delicacy.

Poets were once like knights who sought the Grail. Like *"ducs* in old Roman fashion," they eschewed elaboration and fine decoration in favor of simplicity. The Grail, one assumes, was a kind of pure and honest poetry.

"They did not let self bar / their usefulness to others who were / different." Obfuscation in the service of the ego was not one of the characteristics of the work of these knight-poets. "Heroes need not write an ordinall of attributes to enumerate / what they hate," unlike, for instance, certain poetic movements that spend more time outlining what they are against than writing what they admire.

Miss Moore confesses that she would like to talk to one of these knights "about excess, / and armor's undermining modesty / instead of innocent depravity." Armor in this case seems more like determination than protection. It undermines excess by its will to honest simplicity. She would prefer this sort of conversation to the "innocent depravity," the ignorant corruption, of most talk about poetry.

"A mirror-of-steel uninsistence" is, I think, a description of the poetic mind as Miss Moore would wish it to be. It is both mirror and shield, thus both reflecting and impenetrable. Its "frame of circumstance" is height and solitude and innocence, impenetrability, and it reflects the world. It can "countenance / continence" and it is firmly uninsistent. I think this may mean that it does not insist on its own fecundity, but will accept periods of continence, fallow periods, times of restraint. There could be no better description of Miss Moore's own mind.

There is no particular reason to think this explanation is sound. I think it is at least partly sound, but the poem is too complicated and, in a sense, too private to admit one into all its interstices. The final line defeats me. So too do the lines, "Though Mars is excessive / in being preventive." But that there is something genuine going on is never in doubt.

People say you can tell whether a coin is genuine if you bite it. You can feel real poetry with your mouth. Here we find "the cork oak acorn grown in Spain" and "the pale-ale-eyed impersonal look," "faulty etymology" and "the bock beer buck." Some of the rhymes exist as echoes in the mouth; the mouth remembers the shape of the word. Thus: Illusion / known, owl / well, iodine / Spain. The second word slides into the first word's reverberations, seeming to continue a sound rather than repeat it, like bells heard across a distance.

You know when you read "It was a moth almost an owl" that there is no faking. So, too, can you feel real imagination in wings marked "with backgammon-board wedges" or in "fragrance of iodine." Without any idea of what is meant by this variety of images and metaphors, you can feel certain that there is a real substance that dictates their necessary existence. The substance may be feeling that cannot be reached directly. It may be perceptions best expressed by indirection. It is not especially important that you know what they mean. I feel certain that Miss Moore did not know when she wrote them.

"Armor's Undermining Modesty" can be compared usefully to "In Distrust of Merits." The latter poem was surely written with a thesis in mind. It is essayistic in its arrangement, furnished with newspaper metaphor. "Armor's Undermining Modesty" grows like a plant, one uncurling image at a time until it is all leafed out. The images cohere to a central root, perhaps, but the root has been growing underground, feeding the imagery without seeming to feed.

CHAPTER IX ✌ PREDILECTIONS
AND *LIKE A BULWARK*

✌ THE PUBLICATION of the *Collected Poems* was followed by a year of unprecedented recognition. In 1952, Miss Moore won the National Book Award for poetry, the Pulitzer Prize for poetry and the Bollingen Prize in Poetry of the Yale University Library. She was awarded an honorary degree that year from Dickinson College and, from her own Brooklyn, received the Youth Oscar Award, given by Brooklyn's Youth United for a Better Tomorrow. She was one of twelve Brooklyn residents that year to receive the award from this social agency that awarded its "Oscars" to persons who could serve as inspiration to the 15 thousand young people enrolled in the agency's settlement houses.

Miss Moore spoke before the National Book Committee upon receiving her award, saying:

To be trusted is an ennobling experience; and poetry is a peerless proficiency of the imagination. I prize it, but am myself an observer. . . . In poetry understatement is emphasis. In poetry metaphor substitutes compactness for confusion and says the fish moves "on winglike foot." It also says—and for *it* I had better say Confucius— "If there be a knife of resentment in the heart, the mind will not attain precision." That is to say, poetry watches life with affection.

She quoted from Wallace Stevens' *The Necessary Angel* in defining poetry further. Stevens "put his finger on this thing poetry . . . where he refers to 'a violence within that protects us from a violence without.' " One thinks of deep feeling and restraint and wonders about the "violence within."

In 1953, there were more honors. The National Institute of Arts and Letters awarded Miss Moore its Gold Medal for Poetry. She received an honorary degree from Long Island University. She received the M. Carey Thomas Award and she went for a time to be visiting lecturer at Bryn Mawr. The *New Yorker* published an interview with Miss Moore. *Newsweek* carried an article about Miss Moore, dwelling on her friendship with Jim Thorpe. *Life*, not to be outdone, published a picture article, *"Life* Goes on a Zoo Tour with a Famous Poet." Miss Moore had, in effect, become a celebrity.

In 1954, Viking Press published the long-labored-over *Fables of La Fontaine*, eight years after Miss Moore had begun her translations. In the same year a bilingual edition of her poems, *Gedichte*, was published in Germany. *Predilections*, a collection of Miss Moore's essays, was published in 1955. These are literary essays primarily, reviews of new books, comments on the work of contemporaries and on the work of other older writers whom Miss Moore admires. Because Miss Moore prefers to say nothing if she cannot say something favorable, the essays are all in praise of their subjects. They appeared originally in a variety of literary magazines through the forties and early fifties. There are also several essays written first for the *Dial* and there is the well-known *"The Dial:* A Retrospect," published first in the *Partisan Review* in 1942.

Randall Jarrell has said that Miss Moore's criticism is not criticism really but an inferior sort of poetry, that she can and must make poetry of everything. It is true. Her criticism is unsystematic, depending upon a juxtaposing of observations and quotations so that an overall impression emerges that could scarcely be called a thesis. A point of view it might be called, but even then it has not appeared by being dragged into sight logically. It wafts through the essays like a breeze in which one can, from time to time, smell a familiar fragrance of iodine.

In her predilections on Wallace Stevens, Eliot, Pound, and Auden she tends to quote a very great deal, hanging particularly admired passages together with small exclamations of pleasure or with comments politely suggesting particular things to be observed. E. E. Cummings, Williams, and Louise Bogan receive comparable treatment, the main good things about their poetry simply and briefly noted between quotations demonstrating the point. Sometimes besides quoting from the work she quotes from the writer about his work, in effect letting the subject write his own essay. "I am abnormally fond of that precision which creates movement," Cummings says. Miss Moore writes it down, then quotes four stanzas of one of his poems to show what he means.

There is something refreshing about a critic who sticks so close to what she is criticizing. Too many critics use their ostensible topics to get at their favorite subjects and we find out very little we might want to know. Although Miss Moore's criticism is impressionistic and unaimed, it somehow manages to tell one a great deal about the work under discussion. Only when she decides to take someone to task—Pound and Cummings to be exact—for indecorous language, epithets and the like, is she an obtrusive critic. And then she is obtrusive only because if she wants to cavil about something. One can think of likelier things in the poetry of either man.

Her essay, "*The Dial:* A Retrospect," is a nostalgic delight, written, again, in a rather impressionistic style. A little description of the *Dial* office, a great deal about the people who worked there, some funny anecdotes and a little history are brought together with affection and humor. One might wish for more detail, a little gossip, greater length, but this small essay is all we are allowed from Miss Moore's vast lode of privateness.

In her essay, "Anna Pavlova," commenting on the mystery of Pavlova's magic, Miss Moore says a startling thing: "One suspects that she so intently thought the illusion she wished to create that it made her illusive—hands and feet obeying imagination in a way that compensated for any flaw." She is speaking of Pavlova's power to create illusion in the Death of the Swan and I think she understands the possible method because she employs it herself. When she wrote: "it stops its gleaning / on little wheel castors, and makes fern-seed / footprints with kangaroo speed," she was thinking the illusion so intently that the words became the thing in much the same way that Pavlova's hands and feet became the dying swan's. When Keats spoke of negative capability, he was talking about the same process, I think. To be able to think oneself into something else and so transmit the essence of that thing is, at least in part, what poetry is all about.

In the opening essays of the book, "Feeling and Precision" and "Humility, Concentration, and Gusto," Miss Moore speaks about the writer's craft directly. The first essay is a series of observations on the subject of poetic composition bolstered by examples quoted from the work of others. "You don't devise a rhythm," she writes, "the rhythm is the person, and the sentence but a radiograph of personality." These tense principles aid her composition: "if a long sentence with dependent clauses seems obscure, one can break it into shorter units by imagining into what phrases it would fall in conversation," "expanded explanation tends to spoil the lion's leap," "we must be as clear as our natural reticence allows us to be." She says "precision is both impact and exactitude," that it is "a thing of the imagination; and it is a matter of diction, of diction that is virile because galvanized against inertia." "Explicitness," she says, is "the enemy of brevity." "When we think we don't like art it is because it is artificial art," she writes and we think of the poem, "Poetry" and the much misunderstood line, "I, too, dislike it." She means, of course, she dislikes artificial art, the sort of thing the essay describes this way: "Feeling has departed from anything that has on it the touch of affectation."

The essay mentions Miss Moore's fondness for the unaccented rhyme which she feels promotes "naturalness." She "notices the wholesomeness of the uncapitalized beginnings of lines." A climax is not artificially devised but is "the natural result of strong feeling." She likes concealed rhyme and interiorized climax. She feels "excess is the common substitute for energy."

"Fear of insufficiency is synonymous with insufficiency, and fear of incorrectness makes for rigidity," she says, and, "we must have the courage of our peculiarities."

The essay could be profitably used as a style book for Freshman English, as could the following essay, "Humility, Concentration and Gusto." The essay speaks of those qualities of mind most necessary to writing poetry in particular, but really to writing anything. Humility, here, means a humble and sincere attitude toward one's work. Originality, Miss Moore says, is a "by-product of sincerity." Humility, she says, "is armor, for it realizes that it is impossible to be original, in the sense of doing something that has never been thought of before." This definition of humility-as-armor is not so different from the shield of humility in "His Shield." It will protect one, not only by disarming the criticism of others, but by palliating one's own self-criticisms and disappointments, it seems.

Concentration is used in this essay to mean compression. "A poem," says Miss Moore, "is a concentrate." One might extend the meaning, however, to suppose that the concentrate is a product of the poet's concentration. The final distillation has resulted from the poet's efforts at precision and compression, his avoiding "adverbial intensives," his judicious use or nonuse of commas. The will to compact expression is surely a trait of character, a habit of honest thinking.

A poem thus compressed may have the effect of being obscure by virtue of its very compactness, and this is unfortunate. "How obscure may one be?" says Miss Moore. "I suppose one should not be consciously obscure at all." I like the "I suppose." It is a sigh. Conscious obscurity is evidently seen as a flaw, but as a small one that may be indulged a bit. Elsewhere Miss Moore has said that a poet has a right to expect some effort from his readers.

Gusto is the term of the essay which is most difficult to define. As Miss Moore uses it, it means energy, enthusiasm, sometimes wit and, in general, a crunchy way of looking at the world. She has quoted a letter from the Federal Reserve Board as an admirable example of concentration. She quotes from Edward Lear's "The Owl and the Pussy Cat" as an example of gusto. Gusto she finds in particular words or pleasing phrases in many places. She quotes Christopher Smart: "Impression is the gift of Almighty God, by which genius is empowered to throw an emphasis upon a word in such wise that it cannot escape any reader of good sense." So, too, is gusto. It "thrives on freedom" and finally comes to resemble that informing inner light of spirit that enlivened the sorts of pictures Miss Moore would choose to buy.

The essays of *Predilections* are little single pleasures. Any one gives a flavor of Miss Moore's mind and method. Taken together they bring the insights of several decades to bear on the writing of literature. Anyone keeping in mind the thoughts of the first two essays would write better. Anyone studying the many reviews of poetry would learn a thing or two about literary criticism. With characteristic modesty Miss Moore has said her prose will always be "essays." Finishing *Predilections* one can only wish that she might essay oftener.

Poetry and the auto industry came together in 1955 in one of the most unusual—and charming and hilarious—epistolary exchanges on record.[2] In October of 1955, Robert B. Young, of the Ford Motor Company's Marketing Research Department, wrote to Marianne Moore, soliciting her help in the naming of Ford's new car. Mr. Young's wife had met Miss Moore at a lunch at Mount Holyoke and had, one gathers, suggested to her husband that Miss Moore might be someone who could bring fresh ideas to the naming of the new automobile. Mr. Young wrote, "This is a morning we find ourselves with a problem which, strangely enough, is more in the field of words and the fragile meaning of words than in car-making." He was writing, he continued, to seek the help "of one who knows more about this sort of magic than we."

The new series of cars was to be rather special and Ford wanted a name that would have "a compelling quality in itself and by itself." The name should somehow convey a "visceral feeling of elegance, fleetness, and advanced features and design." The name should flash "a dramatically desirable picture in people's minds."

Mr. Young suggested that she might like to visit the Ford factory and see the new model. He hoped that she would be interested in the project. He assured her that their relations would be "on a fee basis of an impeccably dignified kind."

Miss Moore replied almost immediately. She would like to think about it, she said. She was "complimented to be recruited in this high matter." She had admired the name "Thunderbird" and would find it hard to do as well, but she would consult her brother "who would bring ardor and imagination to bear on the quest."

A week later she wrote again, saying that her brother felt most of the names she had considered were "too learned or too labored," but that she did have one or two that she would mention. And thus began a series of wildly imaginative names, typical Marianne Moore names that might have come from her poetry, complete with arcane scholarship, precision and gusto.

The first possibility was "THE FORD SILVER SWORD," a name suggested to her by a plant that grows in Tibet and on a mountain on the island of Mani, "Mount Háleákalá (House of Sun)." The plant, she wrote, was "found at an altitude of from 9,500 to 10,000 feet." The leaves are silver-white and have a pebbled texture "that feels like Italian-twist back-stitch all-over embroidery."

Another suggestion was for a bird series, specifically a swallow species, "Hirundo or phonetically, Aërundo." Because of the earlier "Thunderbird" Miss Moore thought "Hurricane" might be appropriate, thus: "Hurricane Hirundo," followed by other models in other years called, perhaps, "Hurricane aquila (eagle), Hurricane accipter (hawk), and so on."

She wondered whether she might have a hint about the car's "exciting possibilities." She wondered whether she might have a sketch.

Mr. Young replied that since Miss Moore was interested in the project and since business was business, they must now agree upon a suitable fee for her services.

Miss Moore wondered how Mr. Young had liked the names.

"I seem to exact participation; but if you could tell me how the suggestions submitted strayed—if obviously—from the ideal . . ." Her fancy, she thought, would be inhibited by "acknowledgement in advance of performance." Perhaps if she was "of specific assistance" they could agree on an honorarium.

Ford was not accustomed to doing business this way. Mr. Young wrote that, "It is unspeakably contrary to Procedures here to accept counsel . . . without a firm prior agreement of conditions (and, indeed, without a Purchase Notice in quadruplicate and three competitive bids)." However, he added, Ford seldom had occasion "to indulge in so ethereal a matter as this" and was willing to agree to her wish for an "unencumbered" fancy.

Miss Moore's first suggestions were fine, he said, had not "strayed." They would like to see more. He enclosed sketches, not of the highly secret new model but of something like it that would suggest the feeling.

Miss Moore replied promptly. She had received the sketches, "They are indeed exciting; they have quality, and the toucan tones lend tremendous allure—confirmed by the wheels. Half the magic—sustaining effects of this kind. Looked at upside down, furthermore, there is a sense of fish buoyancy." She thought it might be called "The Impeccable." She thought, at any rate, that "the baguette lapidary glamor" of the thing was a spur to the imagination. "Performance with elegance casts a spell," she wrote, as she has written, too, in explaining her fondness for animals and athletes. One suspects that it was this admiration for elegant performance that attracted her to the Ford project in the first place.

She said that she would ponder further "in the direction of the impeccable, symmechromatic, thunder blender. . . . (the exotics if I can shape them a little). Dearborn might come into one." There followed shortly a list of other suggestions "for the phenomenon." "THE RESILIENT BULLET," or intelligent bullet, or bullet cloisonné or bullet lavolta." She wondered about "THE INTELLIGENT WHALE": "(I have always had a fancy for THE INTELLIGENT WHALE—the little first Navy submarine, shaped like a sweet-potato; on

view in our Brooklyn Yard)." She suggested "THE FORD
FABERGÉ," not to be confused with the perfume of the same
name, but to allude to the original silversmith. She had thought
of " 'The ARC-en-CIEL' (the rainbow) 'ARCENCIEL'?"

She assured Mr. Young that he need not acknowledge her
"memoranda." "I am not working day and night for you; I
feel that etymological hits are partially accidental." She
thought her bullet idea was promising in that it suggested
mercury and, thus, Hermes and Hermes triomegistus and white
magic.

Another list followed:

> "MONGOOSE CIVIQUE
> ANTICIPATOR
> REGNA RACER(couronne à couronne) sovereign to sovereign
> AEROTERRE
> fée rapide (aerofère, aero faire, fée aiglette,
> magifaire) comme il faire
> tonnere alifère (wingèd thunder)
> aliforme alifère (wing-slender a-wing)
> TURBOTORC (used as an adjective by Plymouth)
> THUNDERBIRD allié (Cousin Thunderbird)
> THUNDER CRESTER
> DEARBORN diamanté
> MAGIGRAVURE
> PASTELOGRAM"

and still another:

> "regina-rex
> taper racer   taper acer
> Varisity Stroke
> angelastro
> astranaut
> chaparral
> tir à l'arc (bull's eye)
> cresta lark
> triskelion (three legs running)
> pluma piluma (hairfine, feather-foot)
> andante con moto (description of a good motor?)"

I have no idea how decision-making proceeds at the Ford

Motor Company, but I like to imagine Mr. Young calling
together half-a-dozen of this industry's captains, settling them
around a table and reading Miss Moore's suggestions to them.
Or, perhaps better, I like to imagine a memo containing the
suggestions turning up on the desks of these men among
sheaves of production figures. Piquant imaginings.

With the last list of names, Miss Moore returned the
sketches saying, "My findings thin, so I terminate them." She
felt that she had failed to capture two principles in particular.
"The topknot of the peacock and the topnotcher of speed"
and "the swivel-axis (emphasized elsewhere)—like the Captain's bed on the whale-ship Charles Morgan."

Included in this letter was one name which she included
against her brother's advice, "TURCO TINGO (turquoise
cotinga—the cotinga being a solid indigo South American
finch or sparrow)." She added as a kind of afterthought, "I
have a three-volume treatise on flowers that might produce
something but the impression given should certainly be
unlabored."

I wonder whether there is any significance in Miss Moore's
varied use of capitals and lower case letters in her titles.
Some are all capitals, some entirely lower case. Are the
capitalized ones her favorites?

On December 8, 1955, came one more entirely capitalized
suggestion: "Mr. Young: May I submit UTOPIAN TURTLE-
TOP? Do not trouble to answer unless you like it."

The Ford Motor Company replied with a huge bouquet
of roses, white pine and spiral eucalyptus. The accompanying
card was decorated for Christmas and said: "To Our Favorite
Turtletopper." Miss Moore's letter of thanks is almost a poem.
She says, "to be treated like royalty could not but induce
sensations unprecedently august."

In the middle of January, 1956, Mr. Young replied to Miss
Moore about the names she had submitted, saying that no
decision had been made, that there were suggestions from all
directions and that hers rated "among the most interesting
of all." In November of that year Miss Moore received a letter from Mr. David Wallace (Mr. Young had been inducted

into the Coast Guard) saying that he wanted to report the name chosen for the new automobile before public announcement on November 19. "We have chosen a name. . . . It has a certain ring to it. An air of gaiety and zest. At least, that's what we keep saying. Our name, dear Miss Moore, is—Edsel." Miss Moore replied, "You have the certainly ideal thing— with the Ford identity indigenously symbolized."

The *New Yorker* published this series of letters which it called "The Ford Correspondence" in 1957 after the Edsel, that most pedestrian of Ford products, had made its uninspiring appearance. The letters seemed particularly amusing to people in view of the automobile's eventual name, which was as brilliant as the success of the product. The play of Miss Moore's fancy, her wit and erudition and feather-touch seemed, by comparison, especially delectable.

William Wasserstrom, in a small article called "Marianne Moore's *Dial,*" quotes Miss Moore as saying that the Ford Motor Company's request for help was not really as incongruous as it might seem. She "had long cherished the brand names of things" and "had been exhilarated by the task of helping to decide this one."[3] She liked, in advertising, the possibilities for combining sound and meaning in brand names. So, upon being asked, she combined sounds beautifully while at the same time joining words and parts of words so that their connotations blending or conflicting created a new thing. This is similar to the method of some of her poems in which juxtaposed images set each other vibrating in such a way that the poem, so born, is a really new entity. In a word such as "Turbotorc" the method is fairly obvious. A name like "Utopian Turtletop" takes more thought.

Wasserstrom suggests that had the Ford Motor Company chosen one of Miss Moore's names, it might have been inspired to produce a work of superior quality. Or, rather, he says, less mystically, had Ford produced a better car, one of Miss Moore's names might have seemed suitable. Certainly a name never better suited a car than "Edsel" suited that stodgy machine. But one can only speculate about the power of metaphor to create in its own image.

To Miss Moore, the Edsel was never stodgy, neither in the early sketches nor later in its steel incarnation. She was driven to the auditorium of Marquette University in a black Edsel and remembers, "Nothing was wrong with that Edsel! I thought it was a very handsome car. It came out the wrong year."

If 1956 was a bad year for the Edsel, it was a good year for poetry: Viking Press brought out another collection of Miss Moore's work in a small volume of eleven poems entitled, *Like a Bulwark*. The first poem of the volume, "Like a Bulwark," appeared originally in the *Saturday Review of Literature*, at the request of William Rose Benét, a long-time friend of Miss Moore. Its original title had been "At Rest in the Blast." The title was changed to "Bulwarked against Faith" when the poem was published in *Like a Bulwark*, and the poem was extensively revised. The changes, as is evident in the altered title, were in the direction of an active rather than passive concept of forbearance. The title was changed once more when the poem appeared in *A Marianne Moore Reader* in 1961, and it kept its new name, "Like a Bulwark," in the *Complete Poems*.

The poem begins with an abrupt sentence of a single word, "Affirmed," and continues with a series of compact, tough words that echo the poem's theme of tough forbearance: "pent," "hard pressed," "compressed," "firmed," "thrust," "blast," "compact," "lead."

The subject of all this bulwarking is most likely the poet herself, toughened against the tempest of fate, firmed by resistance to what would destroy her. "You take the blame and are inviolate. / Abased at last." One might expect the line to read, "You take the blame *yet* are inviolate," but the use of "and" where "yet" might seem logical really makes the poem's point. The very act of taking blame renders the poet henceforth inviolate. Once again, it is the theme of the shield of humility. Humility and abasement are the ultimate proofs against damage. And in this complete humility, this strength through weakness, there is a sort of glory which Miss Moore expresses in a military image, "lead-saluted, /

saluted by lead? / As though flying Old Glory full mast."
The humble creature has become a sort of beleaguered fort,
flying a flag, receiving a twenty-one gun salute.

Possibly the subject of the poem could be the poem itself.
The *Collected Poems* ended with a poem that seemed to be
meditating on the art of poetry. "Armor's Undermining
Modesty" admired a poetry stripped of pointless elaboration,
stripped in fact, to its bare and useful bones. This next collection opens with a poem that is a fine example of poetry
stripped to the few words that are not expendable. The poem
could be seen as an object lesson demonstrating the point
of its argument.

Notice the curious shift from third to second person in the
first three lines, from "it" to "you." The shift suggests to me
that two subjects are being talked about, both poet and
poetry, and that what can be said of the one subject can be
applied to the other. (I assume that "you" is the poet, Miss
Moore's customary modesty prohibiting "I" in a poem this
personal.) Thus, poetry, reduced to a hard kernel of precision,
can withstand criticism, changing fashion, time, fate, its
willingness to be itself making it inviolate. Miss Moore has
said she thinks the firm, compact poem has the best chance
of survival; possibly, then, it is "a bulwark against fate."

"Apparition of Splendor" speaks of the porcupine, armored
with quills. The poem is partly natural-history factual, partly
fanciful, and is full of wonderful imagery. The porcupine is
"the double-embattled thistle of jet," the words giving pleasure
to both mouth and eye. The lines, "plain eider-eared exhibit
/ of spines rooted in the sooty moss" give similar pleasure.
The vowel sounds of these lines compose a subtle master-
piece. Other lines that are nice to say are, "as when the lightning shines / on thistlefine spears," "prongs in lanes above
lanes of a shorter prong," "Shallow oppressor, intruder /
insister, you have found a resister." The vowels are the thing
in this poem and the poem is a rather unusual one in Miss
Moore's work for that reason. Compare a stanza of this to
"Like A Bulwark" or to almost any other poem and notice,
how, in general, consonants are stressed.

I am not sure what "Apparition of Splendor" means to say beyond fancifully describing an armored animal, but if I am somewhat confused by this one, "Then the Ermine" baffles me more. Part of my bafflement comes from the style which, like that of "Marriage," is oblique. Images are juxtaposed with no links provided.

The poems of *What Are Years* and *Nevertheless* are characterized by what, for Miss Moore, could be called direct statement. The syntax of the lines is straightforward. There is little Latinate inversion. The juxtaposition of imagery is not abrupt; one can follow the logic of juxtaposed image and metaphor with little difficulty. The result is "easier" poetry. In *Like a Bulwark* the pell-mell transitions of some of the early poetry reappear. The style of thoughtful discussion is replaced by a kaleidoscope of shifting impressions in which Miss Moore hints at the thing she wants to say. At the same time the poetry begins to be less emotional. In some of the earlier poems the method of obscure juxtaposition signalled deep feeling, and extremely emotional lyric passages, albeit obscure ones, appeared. In the poems after 1956 a great many of the characteristics we have become familiar with in Miss Moore's poetry are still present, but the volume of feeling has been turned down.

"Then the Ermine" represents one of the last poems, I think, in which oblique style harbors depth of emotion. It is paradoxical, perhaps, to confess to confusion about a poem's meaning and to say at the same time that one finds emotion there. Logically, if one can detect feeling one should be able to name it. Characteristically, however, when, in Miss Moore's poetry, feeling seems deepest, meaning is most impenetrable. One *senses* the emotion. It is like an electric charge or like the pulsing of the air after a huge bell has tolled. It informs the words with a kind of vibration that is as certainly there as it is impossible to name. Recall these lines from "Marriage":

> Below the incandescent stars
> below the incandescent fruit
> the strange experience of beauty;

its existence is too much;
it tears one to pieces
and each fresh wave of consciousness
is poison.

I don't think one can say what these lines "mean," but that
there is deep feeling here seems undeniable to me.

These lines from "Then the Ermine" are, I think, similarly
obscure, similarly emotional:

Foiled explosiveness is yet
a kind of prophet,
a perfecter, and so a concealer—
    with the power of implosion
like violets by Dürer;
even darker.

The references to "foiled explosiveness" as perfecter and
concealer of "the power of implosion" might all seem to relate to the controlled, the bulwarked poet, but "violets by
Dürer"? And what of the cryptic last line, "even darker"?

Color, the contrast between light and dark, is the metaphor that carries the poem. The ermine, both black and
white, symbolizes the idea, " 'rather dead than spotted.' "
The crow is " 'ebony violet' " and Dürer's violets, too, are
dark. The other central images are of a bat, the creature of
night, seen weaving about insecurely in daylight, and of
Lavater, an eighteenth-century Swiss poet and priest best
known for his studies of physiography and physiognomy,
dark, half-magical sciences.

I think that darkness, here, may be a metaphor for inward-
ness, for what is magical and mysterious inside oneself or
inside one's poetry. It is somehow frightening as well. It is
the well-loved but dangerous thing. Like the experience of
beauty it can tear one to pieces, can explode, implode, and
is yet a prophet in the sense that it carries with it a kind of
magic Word.

These are a few things to say about "Then the Ermine,"
but much more remains that is unexplained. Why, for example,
is the wavering bat like a "jack-in- / the-green," a reference

to a man who hid himself in tree branches as a part of the ancient May Day rites? What can one make of the ambiguity of these lines: "I don't change, am not craven; / on what ground could one / say that I am hard to frighten?" Why the *"palisandre* settee," what does it signify to Miss Moore? I don't know.

"Tom Fool at Jamaica" uses something of the same method of rapid transition, but the poem is all surface, light verse without deep feeling. We move from Jonah and the Whale to a Spanish schoolboy's drawing to Victor Hugo to the race track in ten lines, but there is just enough obvious connection in the things said about these subjects that the transitions are easy to follow. Jonah and the jockey in the Spanish schoolboy's drawing (which Miss Moore reproduces in the Notes) are both hindered by obstacles. No such easy connection is obvious in "Then the Ermine" between, say, Lavater's physiography and a *palisandre* settee.

The notes for "Tom Fool at Jamaica" are unusually helpful. The horse, the racetrack announcer, and the jockey, Ted Atkinson, are all identified, and their remarks, quotations from which constitute parts of the poem, are given at length.

The poem speaks of the racehorse, Tom Fool, whose elegance of performance Miss Moore admires. He is like the athletes of later poems—very good at what he does—and Miss Moore particularly likes the fact that Tom Fool " 'makes an effort and makes it oftener / than the rest.'" This extra spurt of effort marks the champion she thinks. There is, perhaps, a little ambivalence in Miss Moore's admiration. She admires the performance, but doesn't quite approve of the gambling that attaches to the sport. This is perhaps why in the last stanza she shifts to a consideration of other kinds of champions, only to end with the wistful words, " 'But Tom Fool. . . .'"

Miss Moore has said that "Tom Fool at Jamaica" was much improved by a magazine editor's revision. She says the same for "The Staff of Aesculapius," which appeared first in *What's New*, a publication of the Abbott Laboratories. Perhaps the Abbott Laboratory revision is what is wrong with this poem.

It reminds me, in quality, of some of the war poems, full of rather obvious ideas. I think the problem may be that when Miss Moore slants her poetry for a particular audience she writes less originally. She writes much less obscurely as well. We must have obscurity, in Miss Moore's best poems, if we are to have the best poetry.

"Blessed is the Man" was written for the Class Day ceremonies of the Columbia University Chapter of Phi Beta Kappa. Later it was published in the *Ladies Home Journal*. "Rosemary" was published in *Vogue*. Both poems are quickly understood. They are pleasant verse, but with the exception of a line or two, not exceptional poetry. In "Rosemary" I like the lines, "to flower both as symbol and as pungency" and, "it feeds on dew and to the bee / 'hath a dumb language.' " And in "Blessed is the Man" I think the last image, "whose illumined eye has seen the shaft that gilds the sultan's tower," is startlingly lovely.

The poems, "Style" and "The Sycamore," are, by comparison, better poetry. They are, to begin with, more eccentric; they could not have been written by anyone else. While there is in neither poem deep meaning or emotion, there are images that come directly from Miss Moore's unique vision and delight the reader in their minute perfection. For example, speaking of guitar playing in the poem, "Style," Miss Moore describes the technique this way:

> It is as though
> the equidistant three tiny arcs of seeds in a banana
> had been conjoined by Palestrina;

That is Marianne Moore and nobody else—banana / Palestrina, indeed! "The Sycamore" likens the tree against the sky to "an albino giraffe" and speaks of "a little dry / thing from the grass, / in the shape of a Maltese cross, / retiringly formal."

Both these poems fall, in terms of style, between the well-connected "Blessed is the Man" and the unconnected "Then The Ermine." They require the reader to make leaps of imagination, but not mountain-goat leaps. To negotiate "Logic and 'The Magic Flute,' " it seems at first that one will need a parachute, but sooner or later one finds in the Notes that Miss Moore is describing a television colorcast of the opera and much of the imagery falls into place.

She is sitting in her living room "near Life and Time / in their peculiar catacomb," by which she means nothing cosmic as might appear at first glance, but simply two magazines in a rack. She is watching *The Magic Flute* presented on television but is confused by the juxtaposition of operatic presentation and domestic circumstance: "Up winding stair, / here, where, in what theater lost?" She is reminded by the allusion to winding stairs of the Chinese wentletrap, a convoluted shell of which a sketch is provided in the Notes. This seems almost a description of the mind's method of association and, I think, introduces the poem's theme. Television, with its sudden ability to bring a vast array of distant events right to one's feet, confounds and confuses the logic of a lifetime but its magic is congenial to the imagination.

Miss Moore sees at one moment the pale light of a television warming up ("was I seeing a ghost— / a reminder at least / of a sunbeam or moonbeam / that has not a waist?") and at the next, the scene of the opera itself with, apparently, its winding stair reminiscent of the shell. Just as Miss Moore's mind begins a pattern of association—the shell, the living room's "abalonean gloom"—suddenly all logical connections are broken:

> Then out of doors,
>   where interlacing pairs
> of skaters raced from rink
> to ramp, a demon roared
>   as if down flights of marble stairs:
>
> "What is love and
> shall I ever have it?"

These lines must surely parody a commercial, breaking into the middle of the opera and into the middle of Miss Moore's train of thought. Now her mind goes off on a tangent suggested by the commercial. The question it poses brings to mind a little quotation from Ovid: "Banish sloth; you have defeated Cupid's bow."

I think that then her imagination moves linguistically, words play with each other in patterns of association as they do when the unconscious is given free rein. Thus we have "Trapper Love" suggested partly by Ovid's mention of Cupid's bow, referring back to wentletrap and dealing with the question posed by the commercial. "Trapper Love" is a "magic sleuth" (magic flute?) with "noble noise." This composite figure of Trapper Love, assembled out of the associations derived from this "first telecolor-trove— / illogically wove / what logic can't unweave: / one need not shoulder, need not shove." He, not by logic but by wandering association, brings her back to one amazing fact: watching opera on television all alone is possible in the twentieth century, "one need not shoulder, need not shove." Thanks to electronics one simply need not be there.

On one level the poem is simply an amusing account of a reaction all of us who did not grow up with television have had. How can it be possible? and then, how remarkable that it is! The poem is interesting on another level in its description of the associative processes of a mind. We are led through a maze of association by an erudite Ariadne. One thing leads to another and weaves back and forth upon itself. "This," the poem seems to say, "is how imagination works."

Logic is another process altogether. Our logic is shaken by the electronic marvel of television. How can we see *The Magic Flute* in our living room? The logical mind requires a logical explanation in order to rearrange its preconceptions and accept the new thing into its orderly structure.

The imagination is crazy, like television programming. Television can jump from *The Magic Flute* to a commercial and back again with perfect aplomb. The imagination jumps this way. Such disconnection is an affront to logic, but it is imagination's way of life. Imagination sees a crazy underlying connection, be it linguistic or visual, that permits seemingly disparate things to be conjoined.

Finally, then, the poem comes to be almost a discussion

of poetic method. The title might imply that on the one hand there is logic and, on the other, poetry, which itself is a kind of magic flute. Logic progresses on one level, wanting things clear, transitions obvious. Poetry, or imagination, progresses by magic, as music does or as television seems to do, with connections implicit, harmonies felt as much as understood, images coming seemingly out of the air.

I think "Logic and 'The Magic Flute'" is a remarkable poem. It is what it talks about and it talks about what it is, and it does all this with such a light touch and with so much wit. It is a poem that deserves more recognition in the consideration of Miss Moore's work than it has had.

CHAPTER X ᎧᎧᏫ O TO BE A DRAGON

ᎧᏫ FIFTEEN MORE POEMS appeared in 1959 in the volume, *O To Be A Dragon*. Two of its poems, "I May, I Might, I Must" and "To a Chameleon" are very early ones. The former appeared first in the Bryn Mawr literary magazine, *Tipyn O'Bob*, in 1909, and was never reprinted until it appeared here fifty years later. It is a sweet poem that touches me because the poet seems so young and doughty. The other, "To a Chameleon," looks like a chameleon; the type undulates on the page like the poem's subject, twining "round the pruned and polished stem" of a grapevine.

The title poem, a tiny six-line thing, came from several sources. Miss Moore had become interested in Tao, which she describes as a way of life, a " 'oneness' " that is tireless and which she prefers to the "egotism, synonymous with ignorance in Buddhist thinking."[1] Tao led her to consideration of the dragon, one of Tao's primary symbols, signifying the power of heaven. That the dragon could change from silkworm size to an immensity filling the totality of heaven and earth fascinated her in its symbolic possibilities. That it could become, at will, invisible, seemed perfect. She remembers extolling this dragon-symbol once to a friend at a party, and was concluding "a digression on cranes, peaches, bats, and butterflies as symbols of long life and happiness" when the friend exclaimed, " 'O to be a dragon!' " With this exclamation for title and the Tao dragon's symbolic properties for subject, the poem was later written.

Dragonhood is safety, of course, but hardly the safety of humility. It is a symbol of enormous power that can disguise itself in either smallness or invisibility. I think that when one is tempted to take Miss Moore's insistence on humility too literally one must remember the power of the dragon inhabiting the body of the silkworm.

"Hometown Piece for Messrs. Alston and Reese" appeared in the New York *Herald Tribune* on October 3, 1956, during the World Series, and is an exhortation to Miss Moore's beloved Dodgers to win. The poem is provided with plenty of notes so that readers who are not baseball fans, or who are readers who have come to the games since 1956, will not be entirely confused by the variety of players' names and their remarks.

I don't see how anyone could fail to be delighted by this funny, happy poem. It is meant to be sung, one gathers, but I wouldn't try it. The notation is more mood-defining than literal suggestion, I think, and the mood is energetic.

Gusto is what this poem has. It virtually defines the word. I am enchanted with precise Miss Moore speaking of Carl Furillo as "the big gun," asking for "a neat bunt, please; a cloud-breaker, a drive / like Jim Gilliam's great big one." I cannot resist her rhyming of Peewee / superstitiously and harrier / Demeter; nor her statement "Willie Mays should be a Dodger. He should—;" nor the lines "in a strikeout slaughter when what could matter more / he lines a homer to the signboard and has changed the score." It is so incongruous coming from this lady.

I once met an English professor who in former years had played second base for the Louisville Colonels when Pee Wee Reese was playing shortstop for them. Years later, after Reese had retired from his celebrated years with the Dodgers, this man visited him at home and found framed and in a place of honor in his house a copy of Miss Moore's "Hometown Piece." Reese was most pleased by the poem.

And Miss Moore loved Pee Wee. She loved the Dodgers singly and collectively, for how long is debatable. She admits to becoming a "baseball addict" at the age of sixty-six when

she "saw Roy Campanella walk out to the mound to calm
down a pitcher named Carl Spooner." Campanella stood for
a moment talking to Spooner, then "imparted his encouragement with a pat to Spooner's rump as the pitcher turned back
to the mound." [2] Something about the "zest" of that gesture
hooked Miss Moore. Yet clearly she was at least a demi-
addict in 1915, if Alfred Kreymborg's account of her knowl-
edgeability is to be believed—and I think it is.

Miss Moore has explained her affinity for athletes in terms
which, she says, also explain her liking for animals: "They
are subjects for art and exemplars of it, are they not? minding
their own business. Pangolins, hornbills, pitchers, catchers,
do not pry or prey—or prolong the conversation; do not
make us self-conscious; look their best when caring least—."
Perhaps her second pet alligator, which she named Elston
Howard, best symbolized the synthesis of her two enthusi-
asms; although Elston Howard was a Yankee and an alligator
was not her very favorite animal.

George Plimpton wrote an article for *Harper's Magazine*
in October 1964 about the experience of taking Marianne
Moore to a World Series game. He called for her in a
chauffeur-driven limousine, following precise directions, to
her apartment in Brooklyn. She was ready, in a woolen
suit, a black cartwheel hat secured by a hatpin and a very
heavy, very bushy large fur coat. Plimpton notes that the
temperature that day was in the low seventies and that the
coat weighed approximately fifteen pounds.

They set off for the car, Plimpton towering above Miss
Moore's hat. "I would look down on an expanse of black
beret beside me, with only an occasional glimpse of a foot
stepping out from it, or an arm swinging, to indicate she was
underneath. She likes to talk as she moves along and, hearing
the faint hum of her voice under the beret, I would bend
far down . . . to get under the sweep of the hat." He describes
it as quiet under the hat, "like being under a parasol in
summer."

They had a small lunch first at Plimpton's apartment together with Robert Lowell and a few other people. Miss

Moore's lunch was smallest of all. From the buffet table she chose a single piece of cheese.

Then they started for the game in what Miss Moore called the "supercapacious car." En route they talked about sports, football, baseball, and various players. Miss Moore commented that Elston Howard (not the alligator but the ballplayer) could not eat supper if he struck out. Later she commented that Hector Lopez was reliable, "saved many a game, but lacks Cletis Boyer's spectacular uniqueness," and that Mickey Mantle was not graceful, "stodgy in fact, except on a catch way off center."

At the game she admired the mitten used by the usher to dust her seat. She had brought a very small pair of opera glasses with which to view the game. She was interested in the name of the umpire, Shag Crawford. Watching Junior Gilliam at the plate she remarked, "He is simulating *sang-froid.*" Plimpton notes that the man sitting in front of them, beefy and wearing a porkpie hat, turned at this comment to look at Miss Moore, who was concentrating on Gilliam, using her opera glasses.

Some time went by and some plays. Then Dodger Johnny Podres came out to pitch. Miss Moore commented, "Podres affects a great insouciance, but I really doubt he has it." The man in front of them stiffened, Plimpton remembers.

After the first inning Miss Moore's attention began wandering, Plimpton says, then amends it to, "her *concentration* went elsewhere, often away from the focal point of the play." She began concentrating on the bills of the baseball players' caps which she admired. She watched the beer and hot dog vendors with interest. She remarked that a double play is a "cruel thing, but necessary"; that trading players is "scandalous." "I don't know about the traffic in signed balls," she said, "I'd rather catch one."

Some young executives sitting next to her had recognized Miss Moore and had introduced themselves. Now one of them told her that the section in which they were sitting often received a ball from one of the right hand batters. "I'm quite prepared," Miss Moore said.

In the seventh inning it began to rain softly. One of the executives offered his raincoat to Miss Moore. After her demurring and his insisting, she took it, removed her hat, placed it on her lap and carefully covered it with the raincoat.

On the way home they spoke of a helicopter trip she had recently taken as a guest of the Port of New York Authority to see some docks and bridges and part of the World's Fair Grounds. She liked the helicopter, said, "It *feels* its way down, settles in a swirl—like a lady curling a train around her feet before sitting."

She said that she was eager to visit a farm in Vermont where there were some musk oxen. Musk oxen, she said, "love jumping in and out of holes. They've been maligned about their smell—the musk-ox smell—because if you put your nose in one when he's been rained on and is wet, he smells of water, nothing else." She had been invited by the farm's owner to visit but remarked, "Perhaps it's my duty to forget it; too many visitors do become a problem, I believe."

Then they reached her apartment door and quickly she was gone. Back in the car the chauffeur was excited. "My God!" he said, "who was that lady?" Plimpton explained she was a great American poet.

"*Great?* Listen," the driver said, "I had many kinds of customers [he mentioned Richard Nixon as one important one] . . . but she's got them all beat."

The driver hoped she'd liked the game. He thought it was unimportant whether or not she'd understood the score. "It's what she *sees* that counts," he said. "I mean take those oxes, them goats she was talking about. Who would think of putting his nose to a wet ox—I mean that's *great*."

After awhile he said, "Do you think that coat of hers might've come off one of them oxes?"

"The Arctic Ox" is, of course, one of Miss Moore's best-known later poems. Its inspiration came from an article published in 1958 in the *Atlantic Monthly,* by John J. Teal, Jr., the man who later asked Miss Moore to visit his farm in Vermont. The animal instantly took her fancy.

One thing Miss Moore likes about the arctic ox (or goat) is that you need not kill it to have its wool.

> wear the arctic fox
> you have to kill it. Wear
>   *qiviut*—the underwool of the arctic ox—
> pulled off it like a sweater;
> your coat is warm; your conscience, better.

One could have a suit of *qiviut* and later another "since I had not had to murder / the 'goat' that grew the fleece / that made the first." Birds also like *qiviut*, "our goatlike / *qivi*-curvi-capricornus / sheds down ideal for a nest." The arctic ox is, in addition, intelligent and has the sort of cheerful, rigorous personality Miss Moore admires.

The last stanza of the poem reads almost like Ogden Nash:

> If you fear that you are
> reading an advertisement,
>   you are. If we can't be cordial
> to these creatures' fleece,
> I think that we deserve to freeze.

Frequently, in her later poetry, Miss Moore writes a kind of light verse inspired by some current topic that has taken her fancy. A gentle statement of value is usually implicit in these poems. The tone is light and conversational. Armored animals and amorphous fears dwindle away. The things Miss Moore has always valued she values still in these late poems, but her tone of exhortation is gone.

Flannery O'Connor has said that if one can survive his childhood, he has ample material to write about for the rest of his life. Perhaps not if one lives and writes into one's eighties. The themes of Miss Moore's best poetry could not, I suppose, provide the impetus for poems indefinitely. The intensity of feeling associated with the themes must, of necessity, be dissipated eventually if only because writing poetry amounts to a kind of self-psychoanalysis. I think that in both poetry and analysis the reiterating of feelings that one can express even only obliquely leads finally to a sort of purgation. They no longer insist on expression.

Another reason for the poem's progressive outward-turning is suggested by Miss Moore herself in explaining her interest in athletes and animals. She quotes Charles Ives: "The fabric of existence weaves itself whole. You cannot set art off in a corner and hope for it to have vitality. . . . My work in music helped my business [insurance] and my work in business helped my music."[3] Animals, athletes, newspaper articles, museum exhibits, these things are Miss Moore's entrance to reality. They always have been, but in the earlier poetry these bits of objective reality were often the starting points from which she launched journeys inward. In a poem like "The Arctic Ox," the real object pretty much controls the poem, holds it on the surface and in the outside world. Only one stanza of the poem would seem to contain information not available from objective sources:

> While not incapable
> of courtship, they may find its
>   servitude and flutter, too much
> like Procrustes' bed;
> so some decide to stay unwed.

This observation sounds suspiciously more like the Marianne Moore of "Marriage" than it does like an arctic ox.

I asked Miss Moore once about this passage, thinking it must reflect her own ideas about courtship. She replied—obliquely, of course: "David Seabury, the psychologist, said marriage could be a success if each is willing to contribute sixty per cent and expect forty per cent." And, one gathers, thus she decided "to stay unwed."

She has had proposals. In his *Autobiography*, William Carlos Williams reports rumors that Scofield Thayer proposed during Miss Moore's early years at the *Dial*. She herself remembers that her butter-and-egg-and-milk man "affected an admiration" for her. He once asked her, " 'Miss Moore, did you ever think of getting married?' " To which she replied, "Of course. It's brought to your attention from time to time. . . . It's the proper thing for everyone—but *me.*"

There was a little conversation, a very mild disagreement about the value of marriage. Miss Moore concluded, "You don't marry for practical reasons, but for *im*practical reasons."

The butter-and-egg man paused, looked at the ceiling. "I guess you're right," he said.

She tells with delight of an incident that occurred on the Canadian Pacific Railroad. She asked a porter, who was folding her coat inside out against dirt, to do it the other way round. " 'It's the *inside* I want clean. I'm a terrible old maid about my clothes,' " she said.

" 'Well, if you are, miss, it's your own fault,' " he replied.

"Enough," a poem celebrating the Jamestown settlers, has a wry comment to make about marriage: "Marriage, tobacco, and slavery / initiated liberty / when the Deliverance brought seed / of that now controversial weed—" Jamestown's founding, then, was based on a kind of triple bondage and, paradoxically, the settlers were seeking to initiate freedom. Freedom, so far as Miss Moore is concerned, comes, of course, from self-discipline. Marriage, as it is customarily conceived, has always seemed to her to involve a loss of personal freedom.

The poem, "Enough," is only glancingly about marriage. It is really about liberty. It is about the concept of personal freedom that led the early settlers at Jamestown to try founding the settlement. What they did was "enough," "It was enough; it is enough / if present faith mend partial proof." The basic underpinnings of the economy—slavery, tobacco and marriage—may have been misguided from a moral viewpoint. Slavery, of course, implies only selective personal freedom as did the arranged marriages of the settlers. Tobacco is a "now controversial weed." But the underlying idea of freedom that spurred the Jamestown settlers to withstand the hardships of their life is the ideal that Miss Moore celebrates. What they achieved was partial fulfillment of their goal which succeeding generations should seek to make complete.

As is typical of the late poems, "Enough" was inspired by one event or occasion—in this case it was the 350th anniversary observations for the Jamestown settlement. The *Virginia Quarterly Review* commissioned the poem.

On May 13, 1957, three United States Air Force jets named for the Jamestown settlers' ships, the "Godspeed," the "Susan Constant," and the "Discovery," flew nonstop

across the Atlantic from London to Virginia to commemorate
the anniversary. The flight is mentioned in the poem and
serves as a starting point for reflections on the Jamestown
settlement. Again, the poem's subject dominates and controls
expression. The journey is across the surface of historical
fact, the observations Miss Moore makes are from her intellect, not her imagination. The versification is much less intricate than Miss Moore's usual product. The two-line stanzas
are conventionally metrical; the end rhymes are simple—love
/ above, though / go, worst / first, gold / hold.

In discussing Marianne Moore's poems, one comes finally
to the point of having to make decisions—which ones to talk
about, which to leave undiscussed. Because I prefer so many
of the early poems, I have chosen to discuss them at length
and so must mention many late ones only briefly. *O To Be A
Dragon* contains several more poems that are wonderful.
"Melchior Vulpius" is such a one. It was suggested to Miss
Moore by a quotation she found concerning the mysterious
nature of the power a great artist may feel within himself
and yet be unable to name or explain. The poem contains
those lovely lines that describe the act of creation: "slowly
building / from miniature thunder, / crescendos antidoting
death—"

"No Better Than a 'Withered Daffodil' " is remarkable for
the image:

> I too until I saw that French brocade
> blaze green as though some lizard in the shade
>   became exact—
>
> set off by replicas of violet—

All of the precision of imagination that I love in Miss Moore's
poetry is in that image. The same poem contains the lines,
"And I too seemed to be / an insouciant rester by a tree—
/ no daffodil." Here, the elegance of the rhythm is what strikes
me. The way the words "insouciant rester" move within the
line turns the line to slow-flowing honey.

"In the Public Garden" was another commissioned poem,

this time by the Arts Festival in Boston. It was read in June
of 1958. It speaks of the poet as a participant in a public
celebration of the arts among other reflections. I treasure in
particular the way these certain things are said: "Boston has
a festival— / compositely for all—"; "My first—an exceptional,
/ an almost scriptural— / taxi driver"; "a more than usual
/ bouquet of what is vernal." Speaking of Boston she says
she is "glad that the Muses have a home and swans." She is
"happy that Art, admired in general, / is always actually
personal." I suppose the appeal of these lines is their utter
eccentricity of expression. Miss Moore, the person, inhabits
the words, inhabits their arrangements, and the effect is as
individual as a signature.

"Leonardo da Vinci's" is, again, full of characteristic touches.
The poem as a whole fails somehow, and I do not *know* how
exactly. It seems diffuse although it adheres closely to the
legend of St. Jerome as brought to mind by Leonardo's painting. It is perhaps the numerous asides that create a feeling of
confusion, but, on the other hand, it is the asides that are
particularly charming. Speaking of St. Jerome's lion, given
sanctuary in a monastery, Miss Moore says: "The beast, received as a guest, / although some monks fled—." The fleeing
monks are irrelevant really, but noting them makes those lines.

The lion is set to guarding the monastery ass "which
vanished, having fed / its guard, Jerome assumed." Jerome,
Miss Moore notes, was provided "with tapering waist no
matter what he ate." The poem ends, "Blaze on, picture, /
saint, beast; and Lion Haile Selassie, with household / lions as
symbol of sovereignty." Haile Selassie seems a little dragged
in at the end, his Lion of Judah title notwithstanding. The
eccentricity of his inclusion delights me, though. It is the
sort of relevant/irrelevant touch that only a poet writing to
please nobody but herself would dare to include.

Bernard Engel, in his book *Marianne Moore,* traces a spiritual theme throughout the poetry. Its culmination as a specifically Christian viewpoint he finds in the poem, "Leonardo da
Vinci's." Engel says, "The only reliable bulwark for the self
will be acquisition of the powers symbolized by the dragon.

Miss Moore believes that these will come with acceptance of Christ." He finds in the lions of "Leonardo da Vinci's" symbols of Christ, the final mention of Haile Selassie as symbolic of "those who have 'lionship,' a desire for Christ."[4]

I cannot agree with Engel. I don't think Miss Moore's poetry presents sufficient evidence for such a narrowly orthodox interpretation. Her interest in things of the spirit is, I believe, two-fold. She admires those qualities of character that attach to a Christian ethic, certainly. Humility, self-discipline, generosity, honesty, and a general moral uprightness are the values she respects and recommends. They may have derived from religious faith. The relationship may be coincidental. At any rate the relationship is never spelled out.

The other part of Miss Moore's spiritual concern is even less specifically Christian. The mystery, the spiritual substance infusing things, is sometimes noted in her poetry but is nowhere identified as the presence of God. It is, in fact, rather explicitly made indefinite. It is reading in too much to assume that because Miss Moore's ethics resemble Christian ethics, her belief in spiritual mystery is synonymous with orthodox Christian belief. Mystery in Miss Moore's poetry seems to me to be more like the pagan spiritualism of Blake or Lawrence. The source of imagination, "the beautiful element of unreason," can be called the infusion of the spirit of God if you wish, I suppose, but Miss Moore does not say that. Nor does she say that protection comes through acceptance of Christ. She says, I think, that the unnamed mystery exists, that it is frightening, but that is must be accepted if one chooses to create because it is the source of creation.

This is not the Christianity of churches and should not be spoken of in the language of orthodoxy. It is, perhaps, the spirit of mystery that informs all religions in their early unorganized stages, and remains a minor unorthodox—even heretic—strain within some religious orders. It is a recognition of spirit, a celebration of what cannot be directly perceived. A great deal of Miss Moore's most deeply felt poetry can be seen as a coming to terms with this mystery. I think Engel means something like this when he speaks of the acceptance of Christ. It is something like calling a person a Liberal or a Conservative. Naming narrows the possibility for understanding. Too often, when we name a thing, we think we have understood it, and we therefore stop thinking about it. Miss Moore's poetry will not submit to such restriction. The moment we begin to see the journey that Miss Moore has taken in her poetry as a journey toward acceptance of Christian orthodoxy, we lose much of what we might have found in the poetry. To be able to stand not being sure, to be willing to let things go unnamed is the road to understanding. This, in a way, is the struggle Miss Moore has waged in the poetry. She does not proclaim Christ specifically in her verse. She proclaims mystery. She finds protection in being able to let it remain mystery.

CHAPTER XI ✺ A MARIANNE MOORE READER AND TELL ME, TELL ME

✺ IN 1961, VIKING PRESS published *A Marianne Moore Reader* which was dedicated to Hildegarde and Sibley Watson, whom Miss Moore called "particular and very special friends." Watson, of course, had been Miss Moore's close consultant throughout her years as editor of the *Dial*. His wife, Hildegarde, had long been Miss Moore's no less treasured friend.

The volume contains a selection of previously published poems, five new ones, a selection of the La Fontaine translations, a few of the essays from *Predilections*, a choice of "Other Prose" including the Ford Letters, and a *Paris Review* interview. The new poems were later collected in a volume of poetry, *Tell Me, Tell Me*. The "other prose" is a heterogenous group of essays about literature and about life. The Foreword to the volume explains why the book was published (things were out of print, other things needed revision) and comments on questions about her work that Miss Moore is apparently often asked ("Why the many quotation marks?" "Why an inordinate interest in animals and athletes?"). The Foreword contains a bit of political comment, "I am deplored 'for extolling President Eisenhower for the very reasons for which I should reprehend him.'" There are a few ideas about poetry, "Prosody is a tool; poetry is 'a maze, a trap, a web.'" There is everywhere in the book, from dedication to Notes, the same lovely, lively mind at work.

Of the essays, "Idiosyncracy and Technique" repeats many

of the ideas Miss Moore has expressed elsewhere, but which could be expressed a dozen more times with profit. Of technique, she says: "One writes because one has a burning desire to objectify what it is indispensable to one's happiness to express"; "for most defects, to delete is the instantaneous cure"; "writing . . . is an expedient for making one's self understood"; "clarity depends on precision"; "What do I mean by straight writing . . . writing that is not mannered, over-conscious, or at war with common sense." Of idiosyncracy: "An author . . . is a fashioner of words, stamps them with his own personality, and wears the raiment he has made, in his own way"; "genius . . . a combination of attributes . . . three of which are honesty, a sense of the really significant, and the power of concentration."

"Brooklyn from Clinton Hill" extolls the "tame excitement" of that city, describes some of its places and pleasures. "My Crow, Pluto—A Fantasy" is a kind of essay that Miss Moore wrote after attempting a poem on the subject in a two-syllable line, two-line stanza: "I am changing to prose as less restrictive than verse" she says—less restrictive than that *particular* verse form, at least! The essay is a fantasy about a crow, as stated, and slightly too whimsical for my taste.

There is an article of advice for young girls called "If I Were Sixteen Today." There is an article about the painter, Robert Andrew Parker, whom Miss Moore characterizes as "the most accurate and at the same time most unliteral of painters." She describes him as combining "the mystical and the actual" and could, I think, be describing her own work. As she wrote in "Idiosyncracy and Technique," "it is a curiosity of literature how often what one says of another seems descriptive of one's self." There is an interesting essay about Edith Sitwell, whom Miss Moore calls "a virtuoso of rhythm and accent" and who, says Miss Moore, "has also encouraged me in my rhythmic eccentricities."

Miss Moore has elsewhere recollected a visit she made to Dame Edith on a trip to England. As in most of Miss Moore's reminiscences of visits to well-known people, the account is filled with a great deal of description of circumstantial detail and with very little detail about the conversation. One might wish for both. Dame Edith's garden path, her cats, the appointments of her sitting room and bedroom are all mentioned in detail. Dame Edith inquired about Miss Moore's hotel. Miss Moore inquired about "the meaning of adhesive tape on her left forefinger." They talked a little of the Sitwells' castle in Italy and of Sir Osbert who had been absent when Miss Moore visited there. They had tea and the visit ended.

Similarly, a visit to T. S. Eliot shortly before his death is remembered as "ideal." The guests are mentioned and the menu: "little round yellow melons with green stripes, sweet like Cranshaw melons. The roast—lamb—was carved at a serving table by Valerie Eliot. For dessert there was a chocolate in ramekins—slightly bitter—of an ancestral recipe, with marzipan candies in the shapes of flowers and tiny vegetables, coffee and liqueurs in the drawing room." Of the conversation at the dinner Miss Moore says only: "Nothing sombre about this dinner—punctuated by esprit such as 'Wensleydale is not the Mozart of Cheeses.' "

The remaining essays of *A Marianne Moore Reader* are reviews of books as various as Bryher's *Gate to the Sea* and George Plimpton's *Out of My League.* All seven books have interested Miss Moore for one or another reason and the essays are dotted with provocative comments. Of Kenneth Burke, Miss Moore says, "His to me master-maxim is this: 'Truth in art is not discovery of facts or addition to knowledge, it is the exercise of propriety,' " but she also levels at him the familiar criticism, almost the only criticism, of her favorites that she permits herself: "Complaints? With Rabelais and Joyce to brother him, Mr. Burke is sometimes coarse."[1] Williams and Pound have come in for criticism on the same grounds, this being apparently the single flaw that Miss Moore cannot forbear criticizing.

Miss Moore's review of *The New American Poetry, 1945–1960* is fun to read. She goes tiptoeing through the works of such people as Kerouac, Ginsberg and Corso with skirt delicately raised, trying valiantly to find the things that she can admire about them. Poets "specializing in 'organs and feelings' —severed from culture and literature, dogged by redundancy and stench—have a stiff task" she admits since "good content, as Samuel Butler said, is usually matched by good treatment." Yet she can say of Kerouac that he has "unity, a tune and the feel of the mountains," that Corso has "vehemence" and that Allen Ginsberg "can foul the nest in a way to marvel at."

The poetry contained in *A Marianne Moore Reader*, with the exception of the five new poems, was all published in earlier volumes that I have discussed. I have spoken of a number of the La Fontaine translations that appear here and of the essays from *Predilections* that are included. There remains the *Paris Review* interview from which I have quoted so extensively throughout this book that to go into it again here would be redundancy.

The book as a whole provides a fairly comprehensive look at the work of Marianne Moore. Many of the best poems are reprinted. The prose is representative of her elliptic style and idiosyncratic viewpoint. I think the interview provides a sample of her conversational style and the Ford Letters do much to show her very particular mind framed by the conventional and limited thinking of most of the world. In a note at the beginning of the book Miss Moore claims to have included the Ford Letters to "correct an impression persisting among inquirers" that she had chosen the name for the new Ford product, "whereas I did not give the car the name it now has." I don't think it ever occurred to anyone that she did. Nevertheless, the inclusion is a happy one.

I would have chosen to include fewer of the translated fables and several more of the early poems, "The Jerboa," "Camellia Sabina," "The Plumet Basilisk," and "Critics and Connoisseurs," for example, since I think they are among her best and are more important to an appreciation of her work than are the translations. But selections are just that, and this one includes a great deal to enjoy.

In 1962, Miss Moore published a curiosity, a dramatization in four acts of Maria Edgeworth's novel, *The Absentee*. Maria Edgeworth, a popular early nineteenth-century novelist, had written *The Absentee* first as a play which her father offered to Sheridan for production and which Sheridan turned down, saying there were too few Irish actors to play the many Irish roles. Miss Edgeworth subsequently wrote the drama as a novel and the original play was lost. Miss Moore's dramatization of the novel is, thus, in the spirit of a restoration.

It is a comedy of manners that turns on the problem of bolstering the fortunes of an impecunious family of Irish aristocracy by a fortunate marriage. Miss Moore defends the story against charges that it is obsolete by saying that the characters have counterparts everywhere today. She cites Ruskin, Macaulay, and Sir Walter Scott as admirers of the novel. If it holds the attention, if it seems relevant, then it is only incidentally a period piece, Miss Moore says, and is still interesting.

Well, yes and no. A comedy of manners is dated only insofar as it is no longer funny, and it is no longer funny when we stop seeing ourselves and our friends in its characters and situations. Most of the characters of *The Absentee* are still around, but the situation is no longer terribly relevant. To that extent the play seems a period piece. The characters are nearly enough to save it and there are some really funny lines. The play begins with a Lady Clonbrony saying, "Grace says my engraved gourd came from Istanbul. Where is Istanbul?" Another character remarks, commenting on what causes love to flower, "Propinquity! Propinquity, as my father used to say; and he was married five times." A mother complains that her daughter is unusual, preferring books to balls. Her friend replies, "Extraordinary. Yet books and all that are so fashionable now, it's quite natural."

All these lines occur in the play's first scene and, unfortunately, the rest of the scenes do not keep the pace. The plot is intricate and the speeches tend to be long and not always very lively. In general, the female characters have the best lines, being, except for the heroine, Grace, marvellous bitches. The hero, Brian, Lord Kilcullen, is an annoying prig and one finds his long, righteous speeches tedious.

The Absentee begins as a comedy of manners for which one

has hopes. By the middle of the second act it is supporting a good bit of political commentary and by the third act has become an adventure story. The result is loss of focus. The play is asked to do so many things that it can do none of them really well. But, all this criticism notwithstanding, *The Absentee* is not a *bad* play. There have been many worse.

The Arctic Ox, which contains most of the poems of *O To Be A Dragon* and ten others, was published in London by Faber and Faber in 1964. Two poems, "Values in Use" and "Hometown Piece," that appeared in the American volume are omitted from *The Arctic Ox*. Perhaps in the case of the latter poem the subject seemed too particularly American to interest a British audience, although "Baseball and Writing," a new poem, is included. "Baseball and Writing" seems really the better of the two baseball poems, of a more general appeal and similar in its energy and slang. Perhaps two poems on the subject of baseball seemed redundant. "Values in Use" is impatient and snappish. I don't miss it.

Of the ten new poems five had appeared as new in *A Marianne Moore Reader*. They are: "Tell Me, Tell Me," "Carnegie Hall: Rescued," "Rescue with Yul Brynner," "To Victor Hugo of My Crow Pluto" and "Sun." Five more are collected here for the first time.

"Tell Me, Tell Me," the poem of that title begins, "where might there be a refuge for me / from egocentricity." The poet is weary of the super-self-consciousness which examines, dissects, and misunderstands every thought, every egocentric twinge of consciousness. A mind so involved is flat and, one gathers, querulous. In this mood Miss Moore summons Henry James and Beatrix Potter's Gloucester tailor to the rescue; the one for his " 'passion for the particular,' " his inconsistency and contradiction and liking for " 'shadowy possibility,' " the other for the relief of fantasy. Fantasy or imagination on the one hand, the particular world of real objects on the other are, one gathers, antidotes to the torpor of self-absorption.

Miss Moore says that she will flee this "viper's traffic-knot" to "metaphysical newmown hay, / honeysuckle, or woods fragrance." She advises herself in French to hush-up, thinks

she might show some deference to her reader and herself.
The example of James, the story of the tailor, have saved
both poet and reader, she says, "from being driven mad by
a scold."

"To a Giraffe," a poem originally commissioned by the
Steuben Glass Corporation, seems to talk about the same sort
of destructive self-absorption:

> When plagued by the psychological,
> a creature can be unbearable
>
> that could have been irresistible;
> or to be exact, exceptional
>
> since less conversational
> than some emotionally-tied-in-knots animal.

"If it is unpermissible, in fact fatal / to be personal" and
not good to be literal either, must one live only "on top
leaves that are small / reachable only by a beast that is tall?"
Well, Miss Moore says, there can be profound consolations
in the metaphysical. Homer presents a world in which "existence / is flawed," in which uncertainty and striving are
continual. One can live with these things quietly, uncomplain-
ingly and find consolation in a metaphysical view of life.

"To Victor Hugo of My Crow Pluto" is a companion
piece to the essay, "My Crow Pluto—A Fantasy." They appeared on facing pages in *Harper's Bazaar*. The poem of two-
syllable line, two-line stanzas is the one Miss Moore says
she abandoned in favor of prose. The whole poem rhymes
u's or *o*'s, the name Pluto sometimes is Plato, and a good
part of the poem is written in "esperanto madinusa" for
which Miss Moore appends a glossary.

The poem begins with a quotation from Victor Hugo:
"Even when the bird is walking we know that it has wings."
This is true of the crow Pluto/Plato. Even though pigeon-
toed when walking, he has the power of graceful flight. And
so Miss Moore lets him go. The esperanto is their mutual
language and makes the tour de force of the *u*'s and *o*'s pos-

sible because a translation is provided. Well, all right. It is quite a charming tour de force.

"Carnegie Hall: Rescued" is typical of the late poems. Inspired by a news article (in this case an article in the *New Yorker*), in light-verse style, it speaks whimsically of the rescue of Carnegie Hall from the bulldozer. There is in the poem a little of the almost-cute about which I am of two minds. I am instantly repelled by her calling Isaac Stern "Saint Diogenes" and "Mr. Star." I feel similarly creepy about the comment "accented on the 'né,' as / perhaps you don't have to be told." Then I think to myself, "Don't be such a prig" and mean that, too.

"Rescue with Yul Brynner" is similarly topical but is at the same time truly compassionate. Yul Brynner was the United Nations Special Consultant for Refugees in 1959–60, as a preface to the poem states. He also acted the King in *The King and I*. Allusions to his fictional royalty are woven into description of his activities on behalf of refugees and the whole is a sympathetic tribute to Brynner and a compassionate look at the refugees' plight. Yul/Yule are punned together in the last lines, the Christmas spirit and the fairy tale beliefs of children said to come true through the agency of Brynner.

"Blue Bug" is a consideration of a polo pony, one particularly attractive apparently, seen in a photograph in *Sports Illustrated*. His imagined movement on the polo field is likened to a dragonfly, an ancient Chinese melody, Redon, and a Chinese acrobat. The Chinese imagery is apt as "polo" is a Tibetan word for the ball used in a polo game. The poem has the sort of free-association-charm that we have become accustomed to in Miss Moore's poetry. It is, however, like Miss Moore imitating herself. The ease with which the associative jumps are made indicates to me, not that I have grown more adept at following them, but that the imagination at work is less athletic. There is no reason that, at seventy-five, Miss Moore's imagination should not prefer to hop instead of bound. I want only to remark that in "Blue Bug" this change is evident.

"An Expedient—Leonardo da Vinci's—and a Query" is a

poem inspired evidently by Miss Moore's reading of Sir
Kenneth Clark's *Leonardo da Vinci: An Account of His De-*
velopment as an Artist and based partly, too, on *Leonardo da*
Vinci's Notebooks. The poem talks of the man's greatness,
his patience "protecting the soul as clothing the body /
from cold," his peerless artistic accomplishment of which he "made
Nature / the test." And yet he was dejected. Not all his accomplishments could lighten the blow of finding his theory of
mathematics refuted by the theory of continuous movement.

> Could not Leonardo
> have said, "I agree; proof refutes me.
> If all is mobility,
>   mathematics won't do":
> instead of, "Tell me if anything
>   at all has been done?"

One can sense Miss Moore's compassion for the man, can
perhaps detect a feeling of identification with his dejection
in the poem. The poignancy of the poem becomes doubly so
for me when thought of this way. Dejection has not been a
commonplace in Miss Moore's poetry, but in these late poems
it appears in several places—"Tell Me, Tell Me" and "To a
Giraffe" notably. There is brisk rejection of the dejected
mood, merely a mention of its existence before it is cast
away scornfully, but mention is made. One wonders why.
Miss Moore, like the Leonardo of the poem, can view her
accomplishments with satisfaction. They should be enough.
Yet looking back over what one has done is never satisfaction
to such a person. It is what lies ahead, the new work, that
is the source of optimism. Perhaps, at seventy-seven, a poet
cannot believe there will be great new work.

And yet there *has* been new work since 1964. In 1966,
Viking in the United States and the Macmillan Company of
Canada simultaneously published a new volume, *Tell Me, Tell*
Me. The book contains the five new poems of *A Marianne*
Moore Reader, the five additional new ones of the English
Arctic Ox, and eleven new works, eight poems, and three
prose pieces that had appeared in papers or magazines be-
tween 1960 and 1966 and are collected here for the first
time.

The prose pieces are restatements of ideas and ideals that Miss Moore has expressed elsewhere in her prose. It is a part of Miss Moore's strength that her beliefs are firm and unchanging. In these essays she says of poetry and ethics the same things she said two, three and four decades previously, but the effect is not, as it might be, one of calcification. Rather, Miss Moore's reaffirmation of principles long held is vigorous and, somehow, life-supporting. She has not succumbed and she has not compromised. Close reading of the poems would seem to indicate that at one time or another despair was a possibility for Miss Moore. Yet in these late essays she can turn again to her old sustaining principles and find them still viable, still sufficient to her purposes.

"A Burning Desire to Be Explicit," first published in 1966 in the *Christian Science Monitor,* is a defense of her intention to be explicit however obscure she may sometimes seem. Quoting Faulkner she says that writing " 'should help a man endure by lifting up his heart.' " Words must be used precisely, with passion, honestly, if they are to be effective. Her own desire to be precise and honest has, I gather, led to expression that sometimes seems obscure, but this has not been her intention. She has always had "a burning desire to be explicit."

"As for the hobgoblin obscurity, it need never entail compromise. It should mean that one may fail and start again, never mutilate an auspicious premise. The objective is architecture, not demolition." So she says in the essay, "Subject, Predicate, Object," a consideration of what poetry ought to be. "—one thinks of poetry as divine fire, a perquisite of the gods," she says. She prefers a straightforward order of words, an absence of mannered expression. "I like to describe things," she says, explaining why she writes. "Wariness is essential where an inaccurate word could give an impression more exact than could be given by a verifiably accurate term."

"It is for himself that the writer writes" and his consolation and delight come in approximating what he has envisioned. Rhythm combined with "charmed words," a form synonymous with content, these are the materials from which

the poet fashions his delight. "Poetry is the Mogul's dream: to
be intensively toiling at what is a pleasure."

We have heard it all before, technique and imagination,
the top of the mind informed by the mystery that underlies
it. It still applies. It is perpetually new. Poets are always
talking about style and technique, this movement or that.
Miss Moore is talking about poetry. What she says is timeless
because it is not limited to the surface techniques of a new
movement. She speaks, rather, of the fusion of mind and feeling, vision and expression that always has constituted poetry,
and that always will.

"Profit Is a Dead Weight" turns its attention to human
values. Published first in *Seventeen* in 1963, the essay is designed to speak to young people of the principles Miss Moore
has found sustaining. The words *lucro è peso morto,* an expression Miss Moore found in an Italian dictionary and of
which the title is a translation, appeared first in "To Victor
Hugo of My Crow Pluto." The relation between flight and
dead weight, freedom and captivity seems inescapable in the
poem and the expression has something of the same significance in the essay.

"Greed seems to me the vice of our century," Miss Moore
says. The drive for profit is deadening. If greed becomes our
motivating force we lose our freedom. In contrast, Miss Moore
sets the values she prizes: sympathy, a willingness to do to
others only what one would wish done to himself, humility,
usefulness, responsibility, vigor, imagination. She quotes Robert
Frost, saying that every poem is about "the triumph of the
spirit over the materialism by which we are being smothered."
Self-discipline is freedom. Its lack is captivity. The spirit,
like the bird, becomes dead weight when denied flight, but,
unlike the bird, has within itself the power to throw off its
captivity.

Of the eight new poems there is one in particular that I
find very beautiful. The others are lighter, some of them
charming, but not possessed of the depth of "The Mind, Intractable Thing." "Dream" is an amusing poem inspired by a
comment in *Encounter* about academic appointments for

artists. What if a university hired Bach? Miss Moore imagines it. He would be expected to compose for university occasions, although this would be no problem after German masterclasses. Perhaps Haydn might even then beg to be lent to Yale.

"In Lieu of the Lyre" was written for the *Harvard Advocate* at its president's request and speaks of its compliance to the request. "In lieu of the lyre" Miss Moore offers several "nutritive axioms," like " 'a force at rest is at rest because balanced by some other force.' "

"Old Amusement Park" imagines the area that is now La Guardia Airport before the airport was built. The land was an amusement park and Miss Moore describes its relaxed, holiday atmosphere to an imaginary hard-pressed modern traveller. The old park was a place where "the triumph is reflective / and confusion, retroactive." Its modern inhabitant can make no such pleasant claim.

"Granite and Steel" celebrates Brooklyn Bridge, its beauty, its engineering and its symbolic importance as a gateway to opportunity. Its span from tower to pier, crossed by refugees from tyranny, symbolizes to Miss Moore the defeat of greed and "crass priority." It is a "romantic passageway / first seen by the eye of the mind / then by the eye," thus being both dream and realization of the dream, symbol and actuality.

"Charity Overcoming Envy" was inspired by a late fifteenth-century tapestry, Flemish or French. The poem begins charmingly: "Have you time for a story / (depicted in tapestry)?" and Miss Moore continues by describing the scene worked in the tapestry. Charity and Envy face each other on a field of flowers. Envy, though armored in an impenetrable array of chain mail, cries that Charity has hurt him and will hurt him more. He is placated finally, convinced there is no plot to do him harm. The poem ends, "The Gordian knot need not be cut."

The poem says, I think, that Envy and Charity are Siamese twins, two sides of a coin. They are inextricably tangled in a Gordian knot. In every man they exist side by side. There can be no plot to destroy one of them because the existence

of the one depends on the acceptance of the other. "The
Gordian knot need not be cut," it need only be recognized.
The title, "Charity Overcoming Envy," would seem, then, to
imply that Charity can overcome envy not by destroying him,
but by accepting the tangled relationship the two share.

The poems of *Tell Me, Tell Me* remind me most of some of
the earliest ones in *Poems* and *Observations*. They are, like
the early verse, tied to an object and use the particular object as a stimulus for meditation. They travel across the
surface of the mind, not dipping below it as the poems of the
middle period do. "An Egyptian Pulled Glass Bottle in the
Shape of a Fish" from *Observations* is an example of the object controlling the poem's movement. "The Arctic Ox" is
an example. "Old Amusement Park," "Granite and Steel,"
and "Blue Bug" are all late examples of the same kind of
poem. The object's excellence gives rise to various ideas,
analogies, speculations, but the object, itself, remains the
poem's subject.

In poems such as "A Grave" or "The Fish," "The Pangolin"
or "Elephants," "The Paper Nautilus" or "Smooth Gnarled
Crape Myrtle" the ostensible subject, the central object of
the poem, is used as an embarkation point for a journey down
into emotion and mystery. It is the emotion that controls the
poem, dictates its images and becomes, finally, the poem's
real subject.

Because, in Miss Moore's poetry, form is synonymous with
content it is often a poem's style that first hints at what is
going on. As a general rule, the closer Miss Moore approaches
to feeling, the more involuted the poem becomes. The connection between images becomes attenuated, the language of
the poem becomes ambiguous. In the poetry of observation
and intellect the style is considerably more straightforward.
The relation of one image to another is, if not obvious, understandable after a little thought. One can understand readily
why certain words have been chosen to modify certain others.
The style, in short, is available to the rational mind. The
poem can be understood intellectually.

The other kind of poem cannot. It must be understood,

if that word even applies, by the irrational center within the reader. A process not unlike a chemical reaction must take place and the rational, paraphrasing mind has only the most tenuous relation to the process. I think of an arc of electricity jumping between two points, of that moment when two people look at each other and for no apparent reason suddenly laugh—metaphor, but more accurate than explanations.

Consider the common root in the words image, imagination and magic. "The Mind, Intractable Thing" celebrates the "imagnifico," the "wizard in words." The poem is a lament for the dwindling of its powers: "The mind, intractable thing / even with its own ax to grind, sometimes / helps others. Why can't it help me?"

The magic imagination, magician, imagnifico, image-maker understands terror, knows "how to deal / with pent-up emotion, a ballad, witchcraft." These things for which the rational mind has no words that will suffice can be expressed by the magic imagination. It has the power. "I don't. O Zeus and O Destiny!" I want to remark in passing and not insist too much that the pagan invocation here would seem to support my argument that Miss Moore's spirituality is not a specifically Christian thing. Here she invokes a pagan god and an abstract deity as, evidently, the keepers of spiritual power. The imagnifico is strong and unafraid of defeat, "of disparagers, death, dejection." The imagination is, thus, a kind of shield against those things which we know Miss Moore fears. It can go to the irrational place where fears grow and deal with them as Miss Moore's rational mind cannot. This power of the imagination has "made wordcraft irresistible."

The next line, "reef, wreck, lost lad, and 'sea-foundered bell,'" recalls the theme of "A Grave." These things like the "dropped things" which twist and turn at the bottom of the sea with neither consciousness nor volition, are the fears of the mind's underside, the memories too sharp to bear, the feelings too disturbing to acknowledge. The imagination is a king among this flotsam because it is unafraid, is, in fact, nourished by it.

The imagination, thus, becomes like the dragon of "The Plumet Basilisk." That dragon, small but powerful, could dive to the bottom of mystery. I think in the earlier poem Miss Moore was not quite aware that within herself dwelt an equivalent power. She envied the dragon. She knew, I think, that the water of which she spoke had an analogous existence in her own unconscious mind, but I do not believe that at the time Miss Moore wrote "The Plumet Basilisk" she consciously understood that the dragons of the poem could have a parallel in her own dragon imagination. By the time she wrote "The Mind, Intractable Thing," she knew. The poem ends "craft [referring to wordcraft] with which I don't know how to deal." The line might seem to be more of Miss Moore's characteristic diffidence, but I don't believe it is meant that way. I think it means quite literally that without the power of imagination Miss Moore feels unable to write poetry.

This is a remarkable poem when seen in relation to the chief preoccupations of Miss Moore's work. She has always venerated imagination. She has written much about its necessary function, but never has she expressed so clearly what imagination deeply means to her. It is, quite simply, her armor.

We have seen the haunted quality of some of her poems, have wondered why there was such fear and from what source it came. I have suggested that it was the contents of the mind's dark side that threatened beneath the surface of the poetry. How to protect oneself from this unnamed danger has been the obsessive theme of much of Miss Moore's poetry and a variety of armor has been tried. Yet all the time imagination, functioning as image-maker, has been the ultimate armor.

The imagination can go into the place of fears and return with metaphors. It can achieve a purgation without the rational mind's ever having really to know or name the fears that have been touched. Poetry, then, can be like dreams, peopled with old memories and emotions disguised in the crazy imagery of imagination. Dreams protect us. Imagination can protect us, too. It can talk of the mind's obsessive fears in a language of ambiguous metaphor. To face the fears bare of veils would be too dangerous. Yet they insist, persist. They can be looked at slantwise if they wear the costumes of imagination.

Thus, the obscurity and ambiguity that occur in the poems where feeling seems deepest is no accidental thing. Where feeling is deepest, veils are most required. They protect the poet. The obscurity of the imagery is an armor she invents, not as a barrier to the reader's understanding, but as a necessary protection for herself.

CHAPTER XII ✌COMPLETE POEMS

✌ *THE COMPLETE POEMS OF MARIANNE MOORE* was published jointly by the Macmillan Company and the Viking Press in 1967. The book is dedicated to Miss Moore's good friend Louise Crane, and is complete in that it includes all the poems Miss Moore has chosen to reprint. As she comments on the flyleaf, "Omissions are not accidents."

Almost all the poems included in the 1951 *Collected Poems* appear here with the exception of the poem, "Melanchthon." Two poems, "To a Prize Bird" and "The Student" that did not appear in the *Collected Poems*, are included in this volume. Titles are occasionally changed, usually by lengthening, and there are some major revisions in the poems, most of which I have mentioned earlier in discussing the particular poem. The poems "Poetry" and "Peter" are perhaps the most notable examples of extensive revision.

All of the poems of the 1956 volume, *Like a Bulwark*, are included in the *Complete Poems*, with only minor revisions. The major change here is in the title of poem which appeared in the 1956 collection as "Bulwarked Against Fate." All of the poems from *O To Be a Dragon* are included and, again, the revisions are minor; a word changed here and there in the service of precision, some altering of punctuation. Only the poem, "Enough," is revised extensively. Three stanzas are omitted from the original version and one does not regret them.

The poems of *Tell Me, Tell Me* all appear in the *Complete Poems;* the three prose pieces are, of course, not included. There are a number of word changes in these poems, usually happy ones that condense and tighten a poem without altering its content. I regret one change made in "In Lieu of The Lyre." The 1966 version spoke of "a nutritive axiom." *The Complete Poems* version revises this to "a valuable axiom," certainly a revision toward colorlessness. There is one set of revisions that I simply do not understand. The spelling of the esperanto in "To Victor Hugo of My Crow Pluto" changed in every printing of the poem. For example, the word *botto* in *The Complete Poems* was *boto* in *A Marianne Moore Reader* and *beto* in *The Arctic Ox.* Similar respellings occur throughout the poem's three printings.

Nine translated fables are printed in the *Complete Poems,* there is "A Note on the Notes" and, of course, the Notes themselves, and there are four new poems, "Hitherto Uncollected." Of the four, "I've Been Thinking . . ." is light verse in short stanzas speaking of expressions Miss Moore does not like to hear and would never use. "The Camperdown Elm" celebrates an enormous, though sick, elm in Prospect Park, Brooklyn. The tree reminds Miss Moore of Durand's painting, "Kindred Spirits" and, thus, of Bryant and Cole, the picture's subjects, tree lovers who would have loved this tree.

"Tippoo's Tiger" speaks of Tipu Sultan, ruler of Mysore in Southern India, who was defeated and killed by the British. He was a rich and powerful sultan who had a huge toy in which a mechanical tiger killed a mechanical man. "This ballad still awaits a tiger-hearted bard. / Great losses for the enemy / cannot make one's own loss less hard," Miss Moore concludes.

"Love in America?" describes "a benign dementia that should be / engulfing America." Love is like Midas and can transform what it touches. If it were real, unaffected, and from the heart it could be a cure for America's ills. Whatever love is, it is fed "in a way the / opposite of the way / in which the Minotaur was fed"; that is, with gentleness and humanity rather than with the violence of human sacrifice. The title seems to question the possibility of love's existing in America. The last line is an affirmation of its importance.

A few years ago Miss Moore moved from Brooklyn to an apartment in Greenwich Village at the insistence of friends who felt her Brooklyn neighborhood had become dangerous. She has been ill several times in the past few years, but she continues to appear from time to time in unlikely places and to comment on the contemporary scene. The *New Yorker* recently reported her participation at a meeting of the Save Central Park Committee, a group designed to keep park land from being usurped by the city administration's plan to use 7½ acres for a Police Department structure. Miss Moore, age 82, wore her customary tricorn and a green button saying, "Give the Grass a Chance." She contributed a single sentence to the windy proceedings: "Mr. Olmsted [one of the park's designers] was a genius in art, and he wanted the people of the city to get the benefit of nature—a sense of enlarged freedom in limited space." Later in the morning Miss Moore, the meeting's main luminary, was overheard introducing herself to someone: "You don't know me, but my name is Moore."

Time recently ran a photograph of Miss Moore and Mickey Spillane sitting together, in its "People" section. The two were posing for a Braniff ad. Spillane was holding a glass of milk; Miss Moore had just adjusted her skirt. The article reports that someone remarked to Miss Moore that she needn't worry about her skirt, which barely exposed her knees, and that she might have worn her mini-skirt. To which she replied, "I did."

This is the public Marianne Moore, the charming eccentric. There is another public Miss Moore who has received nearly every award and accolade accorded a poet in this country, including, in 1968, the National Medal for Literature for the *Complete Poems*. But it is the private Marianne Moore, of the most private poetry, that interests me most.

There is a poem Miss Moore wrote in 1916 that was published in *Observations* in 1924 and was included again in her last new book, *Tell Me, Tell Me*, in 1966, fifty years after it

was written. The poem was called "Fear is Hope" in 1924. The
title in the late printing is "Sun." There have been no significant revisions except that the late version has the words,
"Hope and Fear accost him," under the title.

This poem seems to me a summation of the miles Miss
Moore has traveled in her private poetic trip toward understanding. Nothing has changed but the title, yet everything
has changed. Fear remains, but the shield against fear, only
vaguely recognized in the early version's title, is named in
the final version. It is the sun, the "imagnifico," the magic-
making power of imagination.

One recalls the final lines of "Leonardo da Vinci's."
Leonardo's sketch seems "sun-dyed." The poem ends with an
exhortation to "Blaze on." One remembers "the startling
El Greco / brimming with inner light" in "The Hero." In
particular one recalls "The Fish": "the submerged shafts of
the / sun / split like spun / glass, move themselves with
spotlight swiftness / into the crevices / in and out, illuminat-
ing / the / turquoise sea / of bodies." These lines from the
early poem seem to me to be a metaphor for the idea that
informs Miss Moore's late poem, "The Mind, Intractable
Thing."

"Sun," too, is a long metaphor. When Miss Moore revised
the title, she drew back a veil so that the late version suggests to me an understanding of meaning of which Miss Moore
was only dimly aware when the poem was written. There is
perhaps no lovelier statement of the power of imagination
in all her poetry.

> "No man may him hyde
>   From Deth holow-eyed";
> For us, this inconvenient truth does not suffice.
> You are not male or female, but a plan
> deep-set within the heart of man.
> Splendid with splendor hid you come, from your Arab abode,
> a fiery topaz smothered in the hand of a great prince who rode
>   before you, Sun—whom you outran,
>   piercing his caravan.
>
>   O Sun, you shall stay
>   with us; holiday,

consuming wrath, be wound in a device
of Moorish gorgeousness, round glasses spun
to flame as hemispheres of one
great hour-glass dwindling to a stem. Consume hostility;
employ your weapon in this meeting-place of surging enmity!
Insurgent feet shall not outrun
multiplied flames, O Sun.

❧ NOTES

Chapter I

1. Introduction to Marianne Moore, *Selected Poems* (Faber and Faber, Ltd., London, 1935).

Chapter II

1. Donald Hall, "An Interview with Marianne Moore," *McCall's*, XCIII, No. 3 (December 1965), p. 182. Except where otherwise noted, subsequent references to Miss Moore's youth are from this source, or from "Interview with Donald Hall," in *A Marianne Moore Reader* (The Viking Press, New York, 1961), pp. 253–275, originally published in the *Paris Review*, Winter 1961.

2. Marguerite Young, "An Afternoon with Marianne Moore," in *Festschrift for Marianne Moore's Seventy-Seventh Birthday—by Various Hands*, ed. Tambimuttu (New York, 1964) p. 70.

3. George Plimpton, "The World Series with Marianne Moore," *Harper's Magazine*, Vol. 233, No. 1373 (October 1964) p. 628.

4. Charles Norman, *Ezra Pound* (The Macmillan Company, Inc., New York, 1960), pp. 210–11.

Chapter III

1. Miss Moore's reminiscences are from the "Interview with Donald Hall," in *A Marianne Moore Reader*.

2. Kreymborg's reminiscences are to be found in Alfred Kreymborg, *Troubadour: An Autobiography* (Boni and Liveright, New York, 1925), pp. 236–45.

3. Williams' comments are taken from *Selected Essays of William Carlos Williams* (Random House, New York, 1931), p. 292 and *The Autobiography of William Carlos Williams* (Random House, New York, 1948), pp. 146–8.

4. This and subsequent quotes from *Post Adolescence* may be found in Robert McAlmon, *McAlmon and the Lost Generation*, ed. Robert E. Knoll (University of Nebraska Press, Lincoln, 1962), pp. 131–4.

Chapter IV

1. Except where otherwise noted in the text, all lines quoted from Miss Moore's poetry are taken from the final versions printed in Marianne Moore, *Complete Poems*, (The Macmillan Company, The Viking Press, New York, 1967).

2. *Selected Essays of William Carlos Williams*, p. 122.

3. Stanley K. Coffman, Jr., *Imagism: A Chapter for the History of Modern Poetry* (U. of Okla. Press, Norman, 1951) p. 223.

4. *Festschrift*, p. 29.

5. *Selected Essays of William Carlos Williams*, p. 124.

6. Marianne Moore, "Ezra Pound," *Reader*, p. 153.

7. *Festschrift*, p. 41.

Chapter V

1. Marianne Moore, *"The Dial: A Retrospect," Predilections* (The Viking Press, New York, 1955), p. 113.

2. This and the following comments, except where otherwise specifically noted, are from William Wasserstrom, *The Time of the Dial* (Syracuse University Press, Syracuse, 1963), pp. 110–114.

3. Footnote to *"The Dial: A Retrospect," Predilections*, p. 103.

4. This and subsequent comments of Miss Moore's are from *"The Dial: A Retrospect,"* pp. 103–111.

5. William Wasserstrom, *A Dial Miscellany* (Syracuse University Press, Syracuse, 1963), p. xii.

6. Wasserstrom, *The Time of the Dial*, pp. 88–89.

7. Moore, "The Dial: A Retrospect," pp. 107–8.

8. Moore, "Ezra Pound," *Predilections*, pp. 68–9.

9. Wasserstrom, *The Time of the Dial*, p. 119.

10. Wasserstrom, *A Dial Miscellany*, p. xxi.

Chapter VI

1. Marianne Moore, "Brooklyn from Clinton Hill," *Reader*, p. 182.

2. Bernard F. Engel, *Marianne Moore* (Twayne Publishers, Inc., New York, 1964), p. 39, and also mentioned in George Plimpton, "The World Series with Marianne Moore," *Harper's*, p. 626.

3. Young, "An Afternoon with Marianne Moore," *Festschrift*, p. 65.

Chapter VII

Miss Moore's comments in this chapter are from the two interviews with Donald Hall.

Chapter VIII

1. Except where otherwise specifically noted, Miss Moore's comments are from the "Interview with Donald Hall," *Reader*.

2. The exchanges between Miss Moore and Ezra Pound are to be found in Charles Norman, *Ezra Pound*, pp. 440–1 and p. 364.

3. *Festschrift*, p. 41.

4. The quotes from LaFontaine's original *Fables* are taken from *Œuvres Complètes de La Fontaine* (Bibliothèque de La Pléiade, Paris, 1954).

Chapter IX

1. *Current Biography 1952*, ed. Anna Rothe (The H. W. Wilson Co., New York, 1953), p. 436.

2. "The Ford Letters," *Reader*, pp. 215–224.

3. *Festschrift,* p. 36.

Chapter X

1. *Reader,* Foreword, p. xvi.

2. Plimpton, "The World Series with Marianne Moore," *Harper's,* pp. 627–633.

3. *Reader,* Foreword, p. xvi.

4. Engel, *Marianne Moore,* p. 150.

Chapter XI

1. *Reader,* pp. 234–6.

✌ BIBLIOGRAPHY

Primary Sources

Moore, Marianne, *Poems* (London, 1921).

———, *Marriage* (New York, 1923).

———, *Observations* (New York, 1924).

———, *Selected Poems* (New York and London, 1935).

———, *The Pangolin and Other Verse* (London, 1936).

———, *What Are Years* (New York, 1941).

———, *Nevertheless* (New York, 1944).

———, *A Face* (Cummington, Massachusetts, 1949).

———, *Collected Poems* (London and New York, 1951).

———, *The Fables of La Fontaine* (New York, 1954).

———, *Selected Fables* (London, 1955).

———, *Predilections* (New York, 1955).

———, *Like a Bulwark* (New York, 1956).

———, *O To Be a Dragon* (New York, 1959).

_____, *A Marianne Moore Reader* (New York, 1961).

_____, *The Absentee: A Comedy in Four Acts* (New York, 1962).

_____, *The Arctic Ox* (London, 1964).

_____, *Tell Me, Tell Me* (New York, 1966).

_____, *The Complete Poems of Marianne Moore* (New York, 1967).

Secondary Sources

The Achievement of Marianne Moore: A Bibliography, 1907–1957, compiled by Eugene P. Sheehy and Kenneth A. Lohf (New York, 1958).

Coffman, Stanley K., Jr., *Imagism: A Chapter for the History of Modern Poetry* (Norman, Oklahoma, 1951).

Current Biography 1952, edited by Anna Rothe (New York, 1953).

Engel, Bernard F., *Marianne Moore* (New York, 1964).

Festschrift for Marianne Moore's Seventy-Seventh Birthday—by Various Hands, edited by M. J. Tambimuttu (New York, 1964).

Hall, Donald, "An Interview with Marianne Moore," *McCall's*, XCIII, No. 3 (December 1965).

_____, "Interview with Donald Hall," *A Marianne Moore Reader* (New York, 1961). Originally published in *The Paris Review*, Winter 1961.

Kreymborg, Alfred, *Troubadour: An Autobiography* (New York, 1925).

McAlmon, Robert, *McAlmon and the Lost Generation,* edited by Robert E. Knoll (Lincoln, Nebraska, 1962).

Norman, Charles, *Ezra Pound* (New York, 1960).

Oeuvres Complètes de la Fontaine (Paris, 1954).

"People," *Time* (February 14, 1969).

Plimpton, George, "The World Series with Marianne Moore," *Harper's Magazine*, CCXXXIII (October, 1964), 627–33.

Wasserstrom, William, *A Dial Miscellany* (Syracuse, New York, 1963).

———, *The Time of the Dial* (Syracuse, New York, 1963).

Williams, William Carlos, *The Autobiography of William Carlos Williams* (New York, 1948).

———, *Selected Essays of William Carlos Williams* (New York, 1931).

———, *Selected Letters of William Carlos Williams* (New York, 1957).

✑ INDEX